W9-BUG-484

OFF THE CUFF

OFF THE CUFF

THE ESSENTIAL STYLE GUIDE FOR MEN
AND THE WOMEN WHO LOVE THEM

CARSON KRESSLEY

Illustrations by Jason O'Malley

DUTTON

DUTTON
Published by Penguin Group (USA) Inc.
375 Hudson Street, New York, New York 10014

Penguin Group (Canada), 10 Alcorn Avenue, Toronto, Ontario, Canada   M4V 3B2 (a division of Pearson Penguin Canada Inc.); Penguin Books Ltd, 80 Strand, London WC2R 0RL, England; Penguin Ireland, 25 St Stephen's Green, Dublin 2, Ireland (a division of Penguin Books Ltd); Penguin Group (Australia), 250 Camberwell Road, Camberwell, Victoria 3124, Australia (a division of Pearson Australia Group Pty Ltd); Penguin Books India Pvt Ltd, 11 Community Centre, Panchsheel Park, New Delhi - 110 017, India; Penguin Group (NZ), Cnr Airborne and Rosedale Roads, Albany, Auckland, New Zealand (a division of Pearson New Zealand Ltd); Penguin Books (South Africa) (Pty) Ltd, 24 Sturdee Avenue, Rosebank, Johannesburg 2196, South Africa

Penguin Books Ltd, Registered Offices: 80 Strand, London WC2R 0RL, England
Published by Dutton, a member of Penguin Group (USA) Inc.

First printing, September 2004

10 9 8 7 6 5 4 3 2 1

REGISTERED TRADEMARK—MARCA REGISTRADA

LIBRARY OF CONGRESS CATALOGING-IN-PUBLICATION DATA
Kressley, Carson.
  Off the cuff : the essential style guide for men and the
women who love them / by Carson Kressley.
      p. cm.
  ISBN 0-525-94836-8 (hardcover : alk. paper)
  1. Men's clothing. 2. Men's furnishing goods. I. Title.
  GT1710.K74 2004
  391'.1—dc22
                                    2004009900

Printed in the United States of America

Set in Dante
Photographs by Matt Albiani
Designed by Richard Oriolo

ACKNOWLEDGMENTS

This book would not have been possible without the generosity and dedication of the following people:

Mom and Dad, Diana, and my entire family.

Darcy Becker and Carlos Ortiz, Ralph Lauren, Jerry Lauren, John Varvatos, Bobbi Renales, David Collins, and Michael Williams.

Chris Brown, Michael Nash, Matt Albiani, JR McGinnis, Dave Metzler, Ben Eskridge, Jen Mendelsohn, Melissa McNally, Jason O'Malley, Richard Oriolo, and Frank Selvaggi.

Jai Rodriguez, Thom Filicia, Kyan Douglas, and Ted Allen.

Kitty Boots, Michelle Platt, and Rachel Pagani.

My team at Dutton: Trena Keating, Emily Haynes, Brian Tart, Richard Hasselberger, Jake "The Flasher" Klisivitch, and Susan Schwartz.

And my family at ICM: Toni Howard, Carol Bruckner, Babette Perry, Karen Sellars, Michael Tenzer, Iris Grossman, and especially Jennifer Joel and Richard Abate.

for **Mom, Dad, & Cher**

CONTENTS

OFF THE CUFF

INTRODUCTION

SINCE THE DAWN OF TIME, MEN HAVE HAD TROUBLE FIGURING OUT

WHAT TO WEAR. IT BEGAN, WELL, IT BEGAN IN THE VERY BEGINNING.

SETTING: Garden of Eden

We hear Eve shouting from stage left.

EVE

Adam, you're wearing that fig leaf . . . *again?*
Are you kidding me? That is so tired!

And so, fashion was born.

And here we are, all these years later, and straight men still have no idea what to wear. Over the last couple of years, I've spent a lot of time in the closets of straight America. Now, I've been in the closet myself for a while, but it was never *that* scary, people.

I'm serious. It's a mad, mad world out there. There are more athletic jerseys than there are men. Polyester is threatening to take over the world. Men actually think they look good in mock turtlenecks and pleated khakis. So while someone else is looking out for the rain forests, I've got to look out for wardrobes across the land.

How did we get into this tragic situation? Well, it wasn't always like this. Not that long ago, the world was a much simpler place because fashion was very regimented.

There was specific clothing for certain things. Most men had uniforms for work, whether it was an actual uniform or a suit and tie, and sportswear for things like hunting and skiing. Like cavemen teaching their sons to hunt bison and make fire, it was a rite of passage for fathers to take their sons to Brooks Brothers to buy their first blue blazer. Fathers taught sons how to tie ties and pick suits and shoes.

And then somewhere along the line—when those pesky cell phones and the Internet became popular?—we became a very mobile society and all those conformities fell by the wayside. Suddenly you could work from your home in your pajamas and fuzzy slippers and nobody knew. (If they did, they probably wouldn't be giving you their money to invest in pork bellies and cultured diamonds.) You could get on a plane in a tank top, ripped shorts, and flip-flops and nobody would look twice at you. Fathers stopped teaching their sons the rules because there *were* no rules anymore.

So we have a whole generation of guys who have absolutely no idea how to dress. And to make matters worse, at the same time there's been an explosion in the number of clothing choices out there, from outlet malls to the Internet. It would be like if you were trying to learn to make a cheese omelet and the only guidance you were given was, "Okay, here are 90 million ingredients. Make something tasty and delicious, but we're not going to tell you how." You'd get frustrated and overwhelmed. You'd experiment and make a lot of mistakes. Like when you thought you were totally cool and bought those acid-washed jeans in the eighties, but it was actually the nineties?

That's where I come in. I'm here, I'm queer, and I can help you. I was going to rescue abused teacup Yorkies, but then I realized there weren't any, so straight men it is! I think they're cute and adorable and lovable, like abandoned puppies at the animal shelter. A straight guy is kind of like a little bird who's fallen out of a tree, until a straight woman or a gay man picks him up and says, "Look at you! You're the cutest little thing! You have a broken wing, but we'll take you to Gucci and you'll be just fine."

So think of me as your very own fashion fairy godstylist, , here to take you on the magical journey to build a better you, starting with an improved wardrobe. I want to demystify the process, because there's nothing to be afraid of. Absolutely everyone can dress well. And it doesn't have to be scary. It's not like you're doing a home pregnancy test here, people. I want to show you that looking great is easy and

Frank Lloyd Wright said,

"Give me the luxuries of life and I will willingly do without the necessities."

I've always been like that. Hmmm. Phone bill or new cashmere sweater? Well, I can survive without a phone. Health insurance or fur? Well, if I have the fur then I won't get sick and I won't need the health insurance. Problem solved!

fun—just like NASCAR and televised bass fishing. Okay, well, maybe not that much fun.

Now, some of you may have seen me wearing some pretty out-there things on TV, and you're thinking, "Why should I listen to *him*?" Fear not. This is all about "Do as I say, not as I do." I wear clothes that are appropriate for my life as a gay reality makeover TV celebutante. I've been known to take my shirt off and go dancing at the Roxy till three in the morning on Saturdays. Most straight guys don't, so my personal style is going to be different from yours. I hope. Or you're going to be in for a big surprise next time you go to San Francisco. I'm going to recommend things that will help you get in touch with your own personal style and make *you* look great.

But before I tell you just how fabulous I can make you, you might want to know just how fabulous I am. Just kidding! But you might want to know where I come from and why I can help you: I was born a poor black child in the parking lot of a Kmart in Decatur, Alabama . . . Actually, I was born and raised in *Allentown*, Pennsylvania. I was practically Amish. Can you believe this much style came from Allentown? Which just goes to prove my theory that it doesn't matter where you come from; it only matters where you're going. Just because you're from a certain place, or you're black or white or straight or gay, doesn't mean you can't become who you want to be. Don't dream it, be it, people! Life isn't about finding yourself, it's about creating yourself!

But growing up gay in a blue-collar town like Allentown—and here's where I get serious for a moment—you realize that you're different, but you don't really know why or how. I mean, when you grow up poor, odds are your parents and siblings are poor, too, so you can go home and commiserate and fight over some government cheese or whatever. But when you grow up gay, you're like, "Why do I have a crush on Lee

Majors and nobody else in the first grade does? Why is my copy of *Dynamite!* magazine stuck together?" You're an outsider in many ways, so you turn a little more inward and focus on yourself a little more. Because you don't have any friends. Ha, ha, ha! (Good times! Good times!) And that gives you a little perspective.

So I know what it's like not to feel good about yourself, and I also know how great it can feel to finally embrace who you really are. That's what I want to help people do—be confident and enjoy who they are. (Are you a jean or a khaki? Maybe you're a Jackie. But that's another book.)

Anyway, I was definitely not born wrapped in a Prada blanket. My dad's in the car business and my mom is the child of dairy farmers in rural Pennsylvania. But the other big influences on my life were my paternal grandparents, who were in the horse business. As we got older, my sister and I got more and more involved in equestrian sports. The horse world is a very, very glamorous one, and one filled with fabulous clothes and rich heritage. By the time I was fifteen, I was traveling all over the United States showing horses at national competitions. I met sophisticated people who lived in big cities. I met movie stars and the heads of major corporations. I met gay people. I was seeing all these amazing clothes that they didn't have at the Chess King at the Lehigh Valley mall. I was like, "Wow, there's something else out there."

After I graduated from Gettysburg College in 1991, I took a job with the Equestrian Federation of the United States so I could move to New York. But after a few years there I learned that man cannot live on nonprofit wages alone. One day when I was working out at the gym in some super preppy outfit, carrying a Ralph Lauren plaid basketball from the holiday '94 gift catalog—I bought something like ninety gallons of fragrance to get it for free—I was approached by a headhunter who told me I was "so Ralph Lauren."

Two days later I had an interview, and in a few weeks I was a gofer for the top executives at Ralph Lauren. (Forever in the back of my brain I'll know that Ralph's brother Jerry Lauren likes his coffee black with two Sweet'n Lows at 6:45 in the morning.)

For the next seven years, I worked for Ralph Lauren and got to see every side of the company, from design and manufacturing to merchandising and advertising. I

The Art of the Tszuj

When I worked at Ralph Lauren, whenever we were styling looks for runway shows or on models, Ralph and Jerry Lauren would turn to me and say, "Carson, give that a little tszuj." "Tszuj it" just means tweak it, finesse it, make it better, make it personal. It might mean paying attention to the details: a little roll of the cuff, a tweak of the collar, or pushing up sleeves. It might be as simple as halfway tucking in a sweater, opening a button or two on your shirt, or tweaking the angle of your ballcap.

The whole reason for tszujing is to take your look over the top. It brings an outfit to life and makes it look like it's not on a mannequin. Tszujing is being alive. I tszuj, therefore I am.

(Tszuj not, lest ye be tszujed!) So just tszuj it, people!

learned about the nuts and bolts of men's clothing: the gauge of a sweater and the thread count of a dress shirt. I visited fashion shows and fabric vendors and design houses. I got really great hands-on teaching from the masters, people like Ralph and Jerry Lauren and John Varvatos. It was such an education, better than I could have gotten in any design school.

Ultimately, I became a stylist in the advertising division. That meant that when Ralph Lauren clothing was advertised in a catalog, I was the fashion police officer styling the clothes, selecting the models, helping with the locations. A stylist is not a designer, and that's what I love about it—it's all about tweaking. It's mixing up the pieces and putting them on a real person to bring them to life. I got really in tune with how you customize looks for different people and different settings. I started doing freelance styling for celebrities. I worked with department stores, helping them lay out their catalogs and style their clothes, putting it all together so it was fresh and fun and inventive.

I still don't claim to be the world's foremost expert on fashion—shocking, I know. But I have had a unique opportunity to get a real education in clothes. I have an inherent ability to say, "That won't look good on you" and "This will look great on you." You may be a software engineer or a waiter or an insurance salesman. There are tax accountants who know every single law and loophole, God bless them. I know all the tricks of the fashion trade. That's my job.

One day in 2002, I was doing a catalog shoot in the Florida Keys when one of the photo producers said she'd heard something on the radio about this new TV show that was looking for all these gay professionals with different areas of expertise. The only thing I knew was that it was being done by Bravo. At that point, I thought Bravo was a nonstick cooking spray. I was like, "Hmmm. I think I have some Bravo from when I made muffins last . . ." Fast forward two years, and now I've made a new career of helping clueless straight men dress better.

Which brings me to this book. This book is an easy, step-by-step guide to help you know what to wear and when, what to get rid of, and how you can shop—whether it's at Neiman Marcus or T.J.Maxx—with the confidence to know what you're looking for. Men's style books tend to be dry and stuffy and serious. I won't go there. You don't need to know who the Glen in Glen plaid is and why he's so fond of this plaid of his. You don't need to know the history of tweed. You just need to know what looks good on you, what makes you feel good, and what helps you get from point A to point B.

I wrote this book for straight men who need it and for the women who love them, but, lest we not forget, also for my gay brethren. Because we all know that bad taste does not discriminate. I don't care if you're gay, straight, or bi, just get some good clothes, for God's sake.

Let's get one thing out of the way, shall we? There's nothing wrong with caring about how you look and dress. It's not at all superficial. To me, that's like saying it's superficial to care about having clean underwear. Or taking care of your teeth. Or going to the doctor. It's just what you should do.

A lot of straight men have been afraid to care too much about how they look, for fear that they'd be perceived as being gay. But now everyone wants to be a metrosexual. Gay is good! We live at a time when the average straight guy has permission to ask questions that he normally felt uncomfortable asking, like, "Does my butt look big in these pants?" and "Are these pleats okay?" (No, by the way) and "Should I get a manicure or highlights?" Questions that guys never would have uttered, they're now asking me at the T.G.I. Friday's in LAX airport. In front of their wives, no less! Times have changed. And I am personally writing you a permission slip to your principal or supervisor or whomever to look good and feel good.

You do have to tread that fine line, though. It *is* superficial to think that if your teeth are whiter and your shirt fits better, you'll be happier. Those things might give you that extra little bit of confidence that will inspire you to achieve. A little taste of looking good can be very inspirational. Suddenly you want to be better the next day, and the next, for the rest of your life. Looking good is just the first step in empowering yourself. And further down the line, everything comes together in a package where the whole is greater than the sum of its parts. It's like my career in math in elementary school: 2 + 2 = 5. Oh my God, I feel *just* like Tony Robbins.

By the way, looking good has nothing to do with how much money you spend or what designer labels you wear. It's not someone coming up to you and saying, "Oh my God! That's a really expensive shirt!" or "Oh my God! Are those Gucci loafers?" It's people coming up to you and saying, "You look fantastic. Did you trim your ear hair?"

Looking good is also not about being "fashionable." When I'm told I'm so "fashionable," it means, "You're so trendy and of the moment." Wrong answer. It shouldn't be about what's hot now and what the newest thing is. It's about feeling confident, and for you, that might mean disregarding what's trendy and "in." Classic personal style is building a wardrobe that suits you and your life and sets you apart from the crowd. It doesn't have to be edgy or wild or look like it comes off a runway. And it shouldn't be dictated by what looks good on models, or what a certain designer says, or even, to a degree, what I say, because it's so very personal. I'm really just a guide, an educator, a medium.

So why *should* straight men take fashion advice from a gay man? Because gay men are generally just a little more sensitive to aesthetics. We pay attention to details. We have all this free time because we're not watching *SportsCenter* or having sex with women. I think that improves our clarity. Just kidding!

Seriously, though, all those years on the playground when all the other boys were making fun of me, I thought, "Oh my God! If only we had something in common!" And now here I am, building bridges, one manicure or trip to Barneys at a time. This book is just my way of reaching out and saying, "This comes from a place of love." Or maybe it's severe adolescent rejection. We're going to get through this just fine if you just hold my hand, and step away from the pleated khakis.

The Ten Fashion Commandments According to Carson Kressley

As we proceed on our magical journey to fabulousness, there are some rules for you to follow. Keep your hands inside the tram car at all times and don't feed the models.

1. **Disregard trends.** You shouldn't wear something just because it's of the fashion moment. You have to be yourself, find what looks good on you, and embrace it, even if it's not "in." Be one with the penny loafer. The biggest fashion faux pas is trying to look like somebody else.

2. **Never underestimate the power of details.** The last thing on is the first thing noticed. Food stains don't count.

3. **Keep it simple, sassy!** For the average guy, it's about building a personal wardrobe that looks great on you. Don't make it complicated. When you have a choice between two items, choose the simpler one.

4. **A garment should never be made of more than 25 percent of an unnatural fiber.** A little bit of polyester isn't going to kill you. A lot of polyester? That's a different story.

5. **Experiment with style.** If you make mistakes, life goes on.

6. **Never go shopping alone.** You've got the store trying to sell you items and you're not sure you look right. But if you have a friend along, you can always get an objective opinion from someone *who knows you*.

7. **Don't overdo it.** You want to be noticed for a look that's yours, and not because you look clownish and inspire the Barnum & Bailey theme song. Overdoing it is like crying, "Oh, look at me!!" I bet you never thought you'd hear me of all people saying that. ("Hi, kettle? It's the pot calling!") I think it's far better to be noticed for subtlety than for garishness.

8. **Never wear anything sheer.** Let's leave the exposed nipples to Janet Jackson, shall we? Thanks for the mammaries, Janet.

9. **Spend within reason.** I encourage many trips to the mall or to your favorite fashion retailer. However, when shopping becomes an addiction, and you have to move every two weeks to flee creditors, you officially have a problem. There are two important things to hold on to in this world: your dignity and your personal credit rating. You don't want to become American Express's bee-atch.

10. **Cashmere is seasonless.** Wear it in winter. Wear it in summer. Wear it to bed and to garden in for all I care, but cashmere is never, ever the wrong answer.

1

Bad Shoes, You Lose:

OR A BRIEF HISTORY OF THE CLOG

WHEN IT COMES TO SHOES, IT'S PRETTY SIMPLE: BAD SHOES, YOU LOSE. AND WE'RE TALKING MORE THAN SELF-ESTEEM, PEOPLE!

We're talking jobs, girlfriends, respect. What you have on your feet can make or break any look . . . and break your toes. Spend some money and get the best shoes you can afford. And for Gucci's sake, make sure that they're comfortable. Because as much as I love sassy shoes, bunions are a real bee-atch, people. Ending up in the podiatric emergency room can ruin Kwanzaa for everyone.

With shoes, it's all about quality, quality, quality. It's better to have two or three pairs of good shoes that will last a long time than to have twenty-five pairs of generic-looking bargain brands. That's especially true of your dress shoes, but you can slide a little on casual shoes and sneakers.

Why does quality matter? Because your shoes are the first thing that women look at, and women (and gay men) know good footwear. You might be wearing the most amazing suit in the universe, but if you're wearing bad shoes, you might as well be wearing a sticker on your forehead that says LOSER.

High-quality shoes are all about construction, and there are a few basic things to look for. Your shoes should be made of real leather and have leather soles as well.

The Fashion Intervention

If you've bought this book for a significant other who thinks he looks fabulous, but his fashion sense is actually stuck in the *Miami Vice* era, you might be nervous about broaching the subject. I subscribe to the Mary Poppins theory: A spoonful of sugar helps the medicine go down. Doing a fashion intervention is a matter of tough love, and as long as you make clear that you come with good intentions, you should be okay. (If that fails, try slipping him a Roofie.)

And if you are that guy who thinks you look super cool in parachute pants and Members Only jackets, you need to listen to what your spouse or best friend is trying to tell you. They care about you and love you, and they want to help. You need to be willing to accept their honesty and candor in the kind, loving way it's being offered. Sometimes you think you look great, but you just don't, and only someone else can tell you that for sure. You need a second opinion. Even I, on rare occasion, think something I'm wearing is amazing and then some good Samaritan—or evil archenemy—will show me a picture of myself and I'll say, "Oh, dear!"

lace-up

wing

Chelsea

flip-flop

If you buy quality leather shoes, they can be refurbished a number of times and will last forever, which is ultimately going to be less expensive than having to replace crappy, poorly made shoes every few months. For those of you animal lovers out there who won't wear leather, I admire your principles, I just don't admire your shoes. Vegetarian leather is like nonfat ice cream. Why bother?

The soles of well-made shoes will be stitched, not glued, to the bottom of the shoe. Also, the lining in better shoes is made of high-quality calfskin or natural leather, not synthetic materials. Finally, check out the stitching. It should be neat and should be barely noticeable.

Okay, so now that you know what quality shoes look like, I bet you want to know what *styles* of shoes you should have. The good news is that there really aren't too many options. (Yes, occasionally that can be a *good* thing.) For women, shoes are

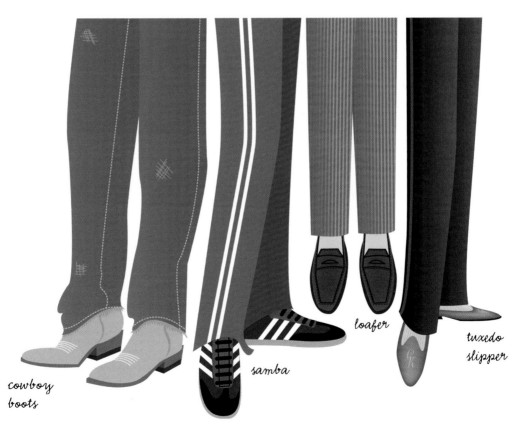

cowboy boots

samba

loafer

tuxedo slipper

velvet tuxedo slipper

patent leather

cowboy boot

snow boot

Birkenstock

military boot

wing tip

black oxford
lace-up

loafer

Chelsea boot

driving moc

samba

more of an accessory, like jewelry, that comes in 95 million different shapes, colors, varieties, and textures. But good-looking, stylish, conservative shoes are an absolute necessity for any man's wardrobe, and there are really just a few basic options for you to choose from.

Shoes are an acquired taste. I'm just going to walk you through the basics (so all you good little straight bunnies need not get overwhelmed on me), because if I unravel the whole world of shoes, you could become obsessive-compulsively addicted to

My favorite pair of shoes are brown suede Chelsea boots with a side gore that get better every time I wear them. They were hand sewn and bench made in England. I just absolutely love them and they look great with a gray flannel suit or jeans. If I ever get scared or lonely I hold them next to me, breathing in their leathery scent, and all is soon right with the world.

shoe shopping. And the next thing you know you'll be hanging out with "gender illusionists" and collecting Cher memorabilia.

I'm not going to bother getting into specifics about the vast sea of casual shoes out there—from monk strap shoes and chukka boots to the whole slew of slip-ons. All I can say is keep it simple, sassy. You can really get in trouble with "fashion" shoes for men.

So here is my list of the ten pairs of shoes that I promise you will take to your grave. (Notice I said that you will take *them*, not that they will send *you* to your grave. Important distinction, people!)

1. **The Black Oxford Lace-up, aka the blucher.** This is the classic lace-up dress shoe (à la the Beatles). And while we're at it, there is no such thing as a dress shoe that is not a lace-up. The black oxford is the perfect complement to all of your dark suits. Just don't wear them with a black suit, because you'll look like a lost Mormon missionary or a Bible salesman. Black bluchers with jeans are not bad as long as the shoe's not too fancy. I hate to see someone with an overdone dress shoe and a pair of jeans. It just looks stupid.

2. **The Brown Wing Tip.** The brown wing tip—also sometimes called a "brogue"—is the ultimate classic shoe. It's a lot like an oxford, except wing tips have little holes punched into the leather in a pattern. Doesn't sound familiar? Think of the opening of *My Three Sons*. Those snappy little tapping toes were wearing wing tips, kids. The brown wing tip looks great with a gray pinstripe suit, as it does with a pair of jeans and an oxford shirt. And who doesn't love versatility?

3. **The Loafer.** As the Judds sang in their country chart topper, love can build a bridge. And a nice brown loafer (penny or tassel—your choice) builds the bridge

The Great Cordovan Mystery

There a lot of men walking around thinking that cordovan shoes—you know, that mahogany, winey-dark color—are okay to wear with a suit. Well let's talk about that, because it's *not* okay.

It might help to take a step back and explain where cordovan comes from. Originally, cordovan was sinewy leather made from a horse's rump. I think you can probably guess how I feel about wearing a horse's ass on your feet. Back in the day when people used horses for farming and work and transportation, there were so many horses around that when they got old and they died, they would use horsehide to make things. Luckily, this is not so popular anymore. Most "cordovan" shoes today are not true cordovan; they're calfskin or leather that's been tanned to achieve what I like to call "cordovanosity." It's a lovely color, but not for your suits.

from sportswear to more dressy clothes. You can wear loafers with a sport coat (but not with a suit) or with casual sportswear—even jeans—and they still look cool and sophisticated in that Marlon Brando kind of way. Do I have to say more than Marlon and Brando? I don't think so. Loafers are also very Italian. In Milan, even the cabdrivers are cool. Why? Because they've got great loafers. And cute little Mercedes-Benz cabs! Who knew?

A word of caution about loafers: Beware the low vamp. No, this is not a trashy woman. The vamp refers to how far the shoe comes up the top of your foot. I hate to see shoes with a low vamp. They are *très* cheesy and they show way too much of your sock. Leave them in the *GoodFellas* wardrobe trailer, where they belong.

4. The Flip-Flop. For five dollars, flip-flops are more fun than an Asian hooker—at half the cost! They're a must-have. Get them in black and brown. Then again, they're so inexpensive, why not get them in every color available? I'm not talking about Tevas here or any other nylon "tech sandal." A technical sandal is about as stupid-looking as it sounds. I'm talking about a plain old flip-flop from J.Crew or Old Navy, or the little Brazilian beauty known as the Havaiana.

In the summer, flip-flops are chic with absolutely everything—shorts and a linen shirt, denim and a blue blazer, khakis and a white cotton oxford. But feel free to wear them right into the fall, as long as snow has not yet fallen and the temperature is still mild. I once wore a brown Jil Sander suit (that's a fancy lady designer from my homeland) with brown Old Navy flip-flops. But this look is not for amateurs. I'll admit that flip-flops are hard to wear in the city and hard to drive in (see The Driving Moccasins, page 21, for those occasions), but that's part of the cachet.

5. **The Cowboy Boot.** The cowboy boot is a classic American icon, right up there with baseball, apple pie, and show tunes. Okay, maybe not so much the show tunes for you. But cowboy boots made America great, and they'll look great on your feet, trust me. Go out and get a pair or I'll kick your ass. Wear them everywhere: in your living room, to a game, to the Emmys, to the opera. They can go everywhere except weddings or funerals, unless a rodeo clown is getting married or has died. Then you're in luck!

6. **The Chelsea Boot.** They're called Chelsea boots because everyone in New York's Chelsea neighborhood, where nearly everyone is gay, owns a pair, and gay men know shoes, people. Chelsea boots are compact boots with a side gore, which is a stretchy little elastic panel that allows the boot to fit snugly even though it doesn't have laces. I prefer them in black, but brown suede is yummy, too. Chelsea boots are classics that go well with absolutely everything—they're

The Glories of Shoe Shopping

Here are some little shopping tricks or treats for your tootsies. First of all, you should try on shoes later in the day, because your feet tend to expand as the day goes on. And make sure you're wearing the socks you're really going to wear—no trying on dress shoes with big white tube socks. Most importantly, don't get suckered by the cute salesgirl who tells you, "Don't worry if they're not comfortable now! They'll break in." Let me tell you a secret. "Break in" is a code word for "Not gonna happen." Shoes should feel comfortable when you try them on. If they're not comfortable when you buy them, they're probably not just going to magically morph into comfortable shoes later on.

Finally, if while on your shopping journey you find a pair of comfortable shoes that you absolutely, absolutely love, and they are so "you," and so great looking—go back and buy a second pair of the exact same shoe. Just like condoms, it's always good to have a backup. Trust me, you'll thank me later.

sexy and a little more rugged than your average dress shoe. And because they were invented for riding, they add just a little equestrian flair to your wardrobe. Trust me, horse people know clothes. It's never a bad idea to copy them.

7. **The Classic Tennis Shoe.** I'm not talking about white Reeboks here. And I'm not talking about all these exotic colored sneakers that make you look like a refugee from the Namibian national soccer team. I'm talking about black, navy, or natural cotton Converse Chuck Taylors, which look great with jeans or a suit. They're always timeless and cool. Think James Dean. If Chucks don't tickle your fancy, try the classic black-and-white Adidas sambas or a chic pair of suede Pumas.

8. **The Athletic Sneaker.** The athletic shoe is where you can knock yourself out. This shoe can be as ugly as you want it to be. (I can't believe I just said that!) It just needs to provide support and protect against bunions and corns. Good times, good times.

Going Sockless

Going sockless can add a WASP-ish, carefree joie de vivre to your look. It's so cool and has a trendy kind of sophistication. I often like to wear shoes without socks from Memorial Day through Labor Day, for the perfect summer chic casual look. But this is only acceptable in casual situations—for those easy breezy summer weekends when you're on vacation or at the beach and it's fun to wear a pair of jeans, a blue blazer, and a white shirt with loafers and no socks. Seeing the tanned tops of your feet can give you all the sexy allure of a Kennedy, without those pesky DUIs.

But going sockless is not for dinner at the White House or for a meeting with your loan officer. In fact, you should never go sockless if you're wearing a suit. This is one of those "Do as Carson says, not as Carson does" times, though, because I confess I have gone sockless with a suit (like on the cover of this book!). But I don't recommend it. At least not for amateurs. Leave this one to the pros.

There is one caveat. If you do choose to take the sockless plunge, you need to use powder in your shoes to avoid your sweaty feet smelling like a cheese factory. Not appealing, people.

Please, my straight friends, do not put taps on your shoes. They're devised to prevent wear and tear on the toe and the heel, but it's really not that expensive to have shoes resoled, and most leather will wear more evenly without them. Not to mention that you're going to sound like some out-of-work chorus line member from *42nd Street*. I only like taps on Liza.

It pains me to have to remind you that athletic shoes are for the gym and for the gym *only*. We're in the midst of a raging sneaker epidemic in this great nation of ours, which has been propagated by the freakishly huge—and growing!—selection of sneakers available. I fear that the number of sneaker styles out there will soon exceed the national population. True athletic shoes, meaning any sneaker that is predominantly white, should be saved for the gym. You can't even wear them to get coffee in the morning. And one thing I really hate to see is men on their morning commute wearing sneakers with a suit. That's a one-way ticket to Tragikestan. It saddens me more than global deforestation. Don't ever, ever do that or, Prada help me, I will personally come and rip those shoes off your feet.

9. **The Driving Moccasin.** A moccasin made for exactly what it says: driving your car. And even if you don't build your wardrobe around driving, you should still have a pair of these, because they're comfortable, they're just plain cool, and they look great with everything. They're especially yummy in chocolate brown and, for the more daring, baby blue. Okay, I confess that driving mocs may not be for amateurs or the average Joe, but who wants to be average?

10. **The Tuxedo Shoe.** If you've made it this far, consider yourself among the lucky. If you already own tuxedo shoes, you probably own a tuxedo. Good for you! I'm beginning to like you already. If you don't, keep it simple on this one and go with a black patent leather lace-up, which is always timeless and classic.

For those who are firmly in touch with their masculine side, most men's fashion books will tell you that the dark velvet slipper is appropriate with a tuxedo. I personally love the formal slipper embroidered with your monogram (or Gucci's or

What Color
Shoes with Suits?

I wouldn't be so worried about rules. It's case by case and you just have to see what looks good. I love a navy suit with a brown shoe. It's very rich and very, very English. I like black shoes with navy as well. Brown goes with pretty much everything but black. If someone tells

Ralph Lauren's), a family crest, or a sartorial nod to a favorite hobby—perhaps martini glasses or a skull and crossbones. (Corporate logos do not count.) Just keep the vamp high so as not to look like an out-of-work ballet dancer.

A word of caution: The velvet slipper is for real pros. In all honesty, I think velvet slippers can be far too gay sometimes, even for me. That's saying a lot, people. Let's just leave it there and move on.

10a. I know, I know, I said ten, but if you live someplace where inclement weather is a factor, you might want some snow boots. Unless you live in Alaska, you're not going to wear them every day, so you can invest in a pair that will last for a number of years. Make sure they look good and they do their job.

Snow boots are necessary because there is no better way to ruin your leather shoes than to walk around in the snow. The salt on the sidewalk will migrate up to the sole of your shoe and cause it to detach. Salt also causes white crystallization on your shoes that you'll have to work hard to get out. (Should you find yourself in that unfortunate situation, try a soft cloth and a shoe cream with mink oil.) If it's

All About Suede Shoes

Whilst I was a student at Ralph Lauren "University," many of my fellow "classmates" seemed to feel that suede shoes were only for fall and winter. I disagree. Many designers are making shoes out of fine, beautiful suede these days. It's so soft, luxurious, and rich that suede has become the cashmere of leathers. And just as cashmere is seasonless, I believe suede—which is inside-out calfskin, in case you were wondering—is, too.

There's also a misconception out there that if suede gets dirty, you have to get rid of it. Caring for your suede is actually really, really easy. All you have to do is get a suede brush, which you can find at any shoe repair store, and give the shoes a good brushing—just like that great My Little Pony you had as a child. Or maybe it was the one you coveted from your little sister. Or was it Pound Puppies? But I digress. Anyway, brush your suede shoes just once or twice a season, and it will extend their life considerably.

snowy out, wear boots until you get to the office or wherever you're going, then change into your dress shoes. Mind you, this is the *one and only* time I will allow you to change your shoes for your commute. Otherwise, it's ridiculous.

Taking Care of Your Friends, Your Shoes

So now that you've amassed this great library of shoes, how are you going to take care of them? It really doesn't take much. You can just literally spit shine them with a soft cloth every once in a while, in between occasional polishings, which need to be done with real, live shoe polish. You don't want to be a slave to your shoes and feel like you have to spit shine and polish them every day. This isn't the Army, people, or *An Officer and a Gentleman*. Oh, don't get me started on Richard Gere. Dreamsville! Sigh.

Your shoes should be kept clean and dry. It's also a good idea not to wear the same pair of shoes every day. Just give them a day to breathe in between wearings and they'll stay with you a long, long time. I'm also a big fan of the shoe tree. Shoe trees are good; plastic ficus trees are bad. If you buy an expensive pair of shoes, I'm going to be very upset if you don't also invest in a pair of $8 shoe trees. When you're not wearing your shoes, trees help them keep their shape and stay fresh and dry.

Keeping shoes in the boxes is always the wrong answer. Your shoes are like trophies. Keep them out so you can see them. I know it's fun to hold on to the memory of that glorious day of shoe shopping, when they all came in their fresh little boxes, but keeping them cooped up doesn't allow circulation, which is really important. Everything in your closet should be able to get some air, as all natural fibers and materials need. I recommend you invest in a canvas shoe holder that just slips over your closet door. That way you can keep all of your shoes out where you can see them. If they are in the boxes, you wind up forgetting what you have and not wearing some. And that would make us both sad clowns.

Always the Wrong Answer . . .

Thick chunky sandals, also known as "mandals." They look good on no one. Never worn with socks, by the way. It's way too lesbian hootenanny.

Wearing socks with flip-flops. Ask yourself, "What would Jesus do?" He wouldn't wear socks.

Anything orthopedic-looking. If your shoe makes it seem that you have polio, it's probably not the right look, unless you do have polio, in which case you should be getting better medical care, as polio has gone the way of the gaucho, people. It's virtually nonexistent.

Backless shoes, otherwise known as the man mule. Always the wrong answer. If you wear mules, you'll look like a jackass. Mules = jackass.

Clogs. One letter away from "clod." Need I say more?

Anything in patent leather unless it's black tie. Or you're a cop. In that case, it's hot. But don't get me started.

Doc Martens. Sorry, all you hipsters, but they're just not polished-looking or classic. They're big and clunky and look like they're meant for working in a coal mine. Attention all ravers: Put down the glow sticks and step away from the Doc Martens. Repeat. Step away from the Doc Martens.

Shoes in bright, crazy hues. You'll look like an ass. Or an elf. Save it for Vegas or the Christmas pageant.

from Carson's Closet

TECHNO CHIC

2

Underthings

UNDERWEAR, T-SHIRTS, AND NAUGHTY SILK TEDDIES. JUST KIDDING!

THERE'S AN OLD ADAGE THAT WOMEN WHO WEAR SEXY UNDERWEAR FEEL SEXY ALL DAY LONG. THE SAME IDEA HOLDS TRUE FOR MEN, as long as you're not actually wearing women's underwear, that is. That's a whole other after-school special. But it's true that everything you put on your body in the morning is going to affect how you feel throughout the day, and if you don't feel good about what you're wearing, it will show. So why not start out by making sure you feel good about the very first thing you'll probably put on in the morning? I mean, it's going to be up in your Kool-Aid all day, for God's sake.

Your underwear is just like my teacup Yorkie or your right hand—it's man's best friend. You want to make sure it's comfortable and it's high-quality. Pulling on those old tattered boxers with the skidmarks or an undershirt with spaghetti sauce on it from a dinner you had during your nanny years will only remind you of that crazy homeless person you saw on your way into work. I want you to aim higher.

The great thing about undergarments is that they're so very inexpensive. So unless you're on welfare, there's really no reason not to get rid of your ratty old ones and treat yourself to a fresh new set once a year—and you can still squander your wealth on other things! And if you are on welfare, pull yourself up by your shirttails, people.

union suit
(1930s)

loincloth
(caveman)

ape

Let's start off by dispelling the myth that it's okay not to wear any underwear at all. Freeballing is never the right answer, except maybe for models. I have one word for you: *chafe*. And that's about as much fun as pulling off a fingernail with a pair of pliers. Not a good time.

No matter what kind of underwear you choose to wrap the family jewels in, it should always be 100 percent cotton. There's a reason they call it the fabric of our lives. It breathes better. It's more comfortable. It's easier to wash. Some underwear might have a little bit of Lycra or spandex to give it stretch, which is fine. Keep it to a minimum, though, because that stuff doesn't breathe as well. You might think that silk underwear is the height of cool, but it so very rarely looks hot on anyone. It usually inspires a giggle, which is not a good thing in the bedroom. So let's leave the silk undies for the ladies and for our friends in the transgendered community, shall we?

domestic partner beater and boxers (1950s)

V-neck and briefs (1970s)

classic tee & boxer briefs (today)

The style of underwear you choose to wear is a very personal decision. Only a few people will see you in this state of undress—your significant other, your doctor, your mom, and perhaps a few bar patrons now and then. (Well, hopefully not your mom, especially if you're over forty.) So will it be boxers or briefs? Well, I believe that boxers are best left to the young and sexy. (Think of the Abercrombie and Fitch catalog. Hold on, let me take a moment to clean myself off.) But a man in boxers who is even slightly overweight or older tends to give off a granddad, nursing home vibe. Save that look for your assisted living years.

Many of you might think that tighty-whitie briefs are the answer. I hate to burst your happy little bubble, but there's nothing like a grown man walking around in tighty-whities to deflate your libido. The ladies know this, and so do I. Now, depending on how lucky you are, you may need extra support while you're working out or playing sports, and that might be the only time it's appropriate to don them. Don't even get me started on jockstraps. They're not underwear, so just let go of your *Vision Quest* fantasies. And as for all the so-called sexy underwear for men—thongs, the banana hammock, anything of that variety—news flash, people! They're not sexy—they're truly frightening.

What I like to recommend is a nice little hybrid number—the boxer brief. They provide excellent coverage, they keep everything nicely in place, and they look sexy on almost everyone except the morbidly obese and the manorexic.

In general, your underwear should be in solid, subdued colors. Underwear's not the place to get creative in your wardrobe. I like plain old white or heather gray, because those won't show up under lighter-colored pants during the summer months and will be

DON'T

novelty boxers   *banana hammock*

useful throughout the year. You might want a couple of pairs of black underwear for your sexier moments. I'm not going to get involved there.

At Christmas or Valentine's Day, you might be tempted to wear boxers adorned with reindeers, cupids, or cutesy sayings. Resist that temptation. You'll only look like a lunatic or a loser. God forbid you have an accident—try explaining those leprechauns on your boxers to the nice male nurse named Terry in the emergency room.

And by the way, theme underwear is out. Was it ever really in? Sure, Underoos had their moment, but you were eight. If SpongeBob SquarePants or anyone affiliated with Marvel comics appears anywhere on your underwear, please get rid of them before some unsuspecting person calls the authorities. If I find them in your underwear drawer, I might have to dial 1-800-ALARM-ME.

UNDERSHIRTS

Think of your undershirt as your dress shirt's little helper. When you have really beautiful quality, super luxurious cotton dress shirts (or even if you don't), you don't want to overlaunder them. If you wear a T-shirt underneath your dress shirt, it runs interference for you by absorbing the sweat, dirt, and body oils that we all inevitably secrete. Yes, even me. By putting a nice little tee under your dress shirt, you might be able to get away with not having to launder the shirt every time you wear it, and your shirt will be your trusty friend for even longer. And it's all about friendships, you know.

If you want to be really chic and you don't have a lot of body hair (or pierced nipples), you don't have to wear a T-shirt, but you're going to have to launder that shirt every time.

I don't care what brand of undershirt you wear or whether you get them at Saks Fifth Avenue or at a store that also sells auto parts and cat litter. The only thing that mat-

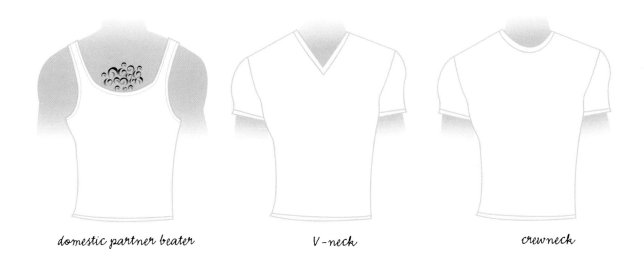

domestic partner beater   V-neck   crewneck

ters is that they should be 100 percent cotton and should have a certain amount of heft to them. Put your hand underneath the shirt. If you can't see your hand through the fabric, that's a good gauge of quality. There are ridiculously super luxurious undershirts made of silk, but there's just no reason for that. No one is going to see them, and you're not going to know the difference. Just good old high-quality 100 percent cotton will be soft and cuddly and you'll love me for them.

You probably already know that undershirts come with different necklines: crewneck, V-neck, and the wife beater, or the domestic partner beater as I like to call it. (You might also know it as the guinea tee. Pause for Sylvester-Stallone-in-*Rocky* fantasy. Okay, then.) If you're going to be wearing a dress shirt with an open neck, I don't like to see the white ring of a crewneck T-shirt peeking out from underneath. I think it's always sexier and better looking to see bare chest. Our European friends know that, and look how they do with the ladies. So invest in some V-neck tees for under your dress shirts. They're perfect: You show a nice bit of clavicle, and they still protect your shirts from sweat and undue wear and tear.

By the way, when I say I like to see a little bare chest, I mean bare chest. I don't want to see your Viagra falls of chest hair spilling out and ruining my day. In that case, you need to become friendly with your local neighborhood waxing professional. (See chapter nine on grooming for more on what I like to call manscaping.) And just please promise me you won't ever wear a V-neck without the shirt on top of it. If you go out in a V-neck T-shirt alone, you will remain that way—alone—for the rest of the night. Perhaps for the rest of your life. Ah, loneliness. Strong medicine.

Though I don't like to see a crewneck T-shirt under an open woven shirt, crewnecks do lend a certain J.Crew, collegiate feel to any outfit. But if you must, crewneck tees should always be white. Gray and oatmeal are a no. They just look dirty. Crewneck tees are great for wearing under a sweater or a sport shirt. But notice I said *under*. The kind of white T-shirt you can wear with jeans and nothing else is not the same kind you find in the underwear aisle at Target for $10 a pack of three. (See chapter four for more on T-shirts.) Just wait till I get my Hanes on you if I see you wearing underwear in lieu of real clothing.

As for the domestic partner beater, these have become obsolete, and they might as well be eradicated. They fulfill no purpose as they don't cover the areas where you sweat the most, your armpits. They just make you look like a refugee from *The Sopranos*, which is a great show, but not where you should be getting your fashion inspiration. But if you absolutely must wear a domestic partner beater, please don't wear them by themselves with jeans. Not unless you're Antonio Sabato, Jr. For him I'll make an exception. While we're at it, I don't think there's a place in this world for tank tops except at the gym, where I kind of like them. In fact I encourage them. There's nothing nicer than seeing a meaty delt out on display with a darling gym ensemble.

SOCKS

Men seem to be eternally bewildered about what color their socks are supposed to be. It's okay. I'm here for you. First of all, it's always better to stray on the side of darker socks, meaning your socks can be darker than your suit. Promise me you will never, ever—*ever*—buy flesh-toned socks. You'll look like you're wearing nude panty hose and just those three words—*nude panty hose*—give me the heebie-jeebies. When in doubt, match your sock color to that of your shoes; it will create a seamless line. You don't want to match socks to pants, because you could wind up looking like you're wearing stirrup pants. Basically, if you buy yourself an army of black and brown cotton or silk dress socks, you'll be just fine. If you want to try some patterned socks, remember to keep it simple. There's nothing worse than a bold-patterned suit with a patterned sock.

Socks can really invigorate your wardrobe. If you're wearing casual clothes, you can mix it up with argyles, herringbone, dots, whatever. Go ahead and have yourself a little party in your shoes. It can also be really festive to wear brightly colored socks—purple, red, yellow, etc.—for occasions like holiday parties, but I say that with extreme caution because this can easily backfire. And just like underwear, any kind of novelty socks (sports figures, superheroes, Valentine's cupids, Christmas trees, socks that play music, light up, etc.) are to be avoided at all costs. You should also steer clear of any sock that's provided free of charge, especially airline socks.

Some people like wool socks for when it's nippy out, but I think most wool socks are scratchy, hot, and tend to trap moisture. They've gone the way of the milkman. They're outdated. For the ultimate in sock luxury, you can invest in a pair of soft and cuddly cashmere socks. They'll probably run you around $150, but you didn't really need to eat much this month, did you? If you can't afford cashmere socks, you can try a merino wool sock, which is a very high-quality wool, or a wool/cashmere blend. It's almost like the real thing. Just like that nice "lady," Suzy, you met at the Vince Lombardi service area on the New Jersey Turnpike! You remember her!

And now we come to one of the pressing questions of our times: How high should your socks be? A good quality dress sock should always be long. They shouldn't be as long as control-top panty hose, of course, but they should always be long enough to go well up to your calf. I do not want to see the gap between your sock and your pants when you cross your legs. First of all, hopefully your pants will not be that short to start with. (Clam diggers are always the wrong answer.) Your socks should also be able to stay up without Levitra. If your socks are falling down around your ankles, making you look like you have elephantiasis, or you're wondering where you can find yourself a good pair of sock garters like your great-grandfather Ebenezer wore, it's time to get new socks. High-quality socks of the proper length should come up to your calf and stay there.

The only exception to that rule is the athletic sock, which is a fluffy white cotton sock to be worn with an athletic shoe at the gym. Period. These socks should be shorter. You don't want to look like a jackass with big tall tube socks up to your knees, like Kristy McNichol wore in *Little Darlings*. It's not 1979, people.

Always the Wrong Answer . . .

Ronald McDonald, Mickey Mouse, or any character underwear. If there's any chance that the character on your underwear is also on your seven-year-old nephew's underwear, steer clear.

Banana hammocks

Flesh-colored socks

100 percent nylon socks

Toe socks

Women's hosiery

Socks that make noise (e.g., play "Jingle Bells" or your college fight song) or light up. In fact, any sock that requires a battery should be avoided.

Chest hair spilling out and ruining my day. Become friendly with your local neighborhood waxing professional.

Big tall tube socks up to your knees, like Kristy McNichol wore in *Little Darlings.*

CHAPTER 3

The Devil Wears Pleated Khakis

THE WIDE WORLD OF PANTS, SHORTS, AND SWIMWEAR

WE COULD TALK ABOUT PANTS ALL DAY LONG. OKAY, MAYBE *I* COULD TALK ABOUT PANTS ALL DAY LONG. BUT EITHER WAY, IT'S important that you know how to cover your ass . . . without making an ass of *yourself*. This chapter will get you through the trauma of finding pants, shorts, and swimwear.

In most work environments, it's not just casual Friday anymore—it's casual Monday, Tuesday, Wednesday, Thursday. If you're not wearing a suit every day, regular pants are going to be the foundation of your wardrobe. That also means they're not the place to get crazy. You can have fun with your shirts, throw on a tie or a sweater or a snappy sport coat. That's all great. But when it comes to pants, it's always better to keep it simple.

Before we go even one step further, we need to talk about pleats. I'm on a mission to eradicate pleated pants in America. Pleats are always the wrong answer, except for a few very specific exceptions that I'll get to in a minute. I don't care who you are—short, tall, big, or small—there's never a reason for pleats, and even after seventeen gimlets, you won't convince me otherwise.

I understand why you might *think* that pleats work best for you. Here's why they don't.

pleats are bad

*flat fronts
are good*

When having your pants tailored, do not look down at the hem, the tailor, or your feet, as almost everyone is tempted to do. It will most certainly throw off your posture and foul up your alteration. Keep your eyes forward at all times.

MYTH #1 *Wearing pleated pants will camouflage a spare tire.* That is just not true. All pleats do is add extra fabric and bulk to your midsection, so they can actually *increase* the width around your middle. They don't hide a spare tire, they just draw unwelcome attention to that area. News fuh-lash! You are not fooling anyone, big guy!

MYTH #2 *Pleats are roomier.* Well, pleated pants are technically roomier, but that's deceptive. Pleats create a little more roominess *below* the waist, which only encourages you to put too much stuff in your pockets and look even bulkier. Men in *pleated* pants look like they're retaining water. Or they're the Michelin Man. Not so much my favorite looks. Pleats also give more room for ugly lumps and bulges, and there's only one bulge we want to see. And even then I don't want to see your bulge. Let's leave some mystique for the ladies, shall we?

The moral of the story is that a plain flat-front pant will always look more sophisticated and cleaner than a pleated pant. Flat-fronts give a slimming effect—there's not as much fabric clinging and pulling. Even if you're a little overweight, it's nicer to have a nice, simple flat-front pant. It's smooth and won't draw the eye to the problem area. Also, dark colors are doubly effective at making you look more svelte.

The only time pleats are acceptable (are you listening, people?) is when they're part of an old Hollywood glamour kind of suit, by a designer like Ralph Lauren, Brooks Brothers, etc. The pleats tie into the heritage of the suit. Other than that, there's just no reason for them. Ever.

Do not be fooled by the many pleated dress and casual pants you will find at even the best stores. They are there because people buy them, not because they look good.

Please let's stop the vicious cycle—don't buy them. Thinking about the pleated pants situation makes me feel like the unhappy Indian chief in the anti-littering campaigns of the seventies, standing on a heap of garbage with one single, sad, glycerine tear running down his leathery sun-damaged cheek.

Okay, I've styled it out and I feel so much better now that that's out in the open. Don't you? Okay. Let's move on to the other ways pants should— and shouldn't—fit.

Length

When we're talking casual pants, I like to see little or no break, which means that the pants should cover the top of your shoe when you're standing. We should not see excess fabric pooling around the ankles, nor should there be an Urkel-esque overexposure of sock. This keeps pants looking neat and smart. If they're really, really long and you're dragging them on the ground, you're just going to look dirty and schlubby and unkempt, and you'll ruin your pants.

For dress pants, I also like very little break, but leave it up to your tailor. The hems should be slightly angled, so that the front of the pant is a smidge shorter than the back. You want the front to land just on or above your shoe, and you want the back of the hem to just touch the top of the heel of your shoe. That means your pants should cover the entire back of your shoe, except the heel.

Most good quality dress pants are going to have unfinished bottoms. I know that sounds naughty, but it just means you'll have to have them hemmed. For dress pants, I like a nice clean hem with no cuff. Cuffs generally belong with pleated pants and we know how I feel about those—unless we're talking about certain suit cuts. (See chapter five.) A non-cuffed dress pant is just a little cleaner, a little more modern, and I think a little more sophisticated. And do not, under any circumstances, let me catch any cuffs on the bottoms of your casual pants, or I'll put you in handcuffs.

Waist

The waist of your pants should fit comfortably, not super tight or snug. You should be able to fit two fingers easily in the waistband.

It's also important that your pants sit at the right level on your waist. If they don't, you can't have them tailored properly, especially if it's a suit or a dress pant. Guys don't know where to wear their pants. Some of them have them pulled up to the sky, and others have them so low they look like a "gangsta."

More than any other pants, it's essential that dress pants fit on your true waist or higher. This means that when you try them on, the waistband should fit above the hip bone, but not touching the belly button. Dress pants should not be low slung, low rise, low anything. Denim jeans should be worn low slung on the hip bone, but not so low we see your pubes.

A lot of guys think that the fit of pants ends with length and waist. Surprise! They also need to fit you in the rise and the seat.

Rise

Ther rise is the distance from the top button to your, um, "taint." (You know—t'aint your ass and it t'aint your . . . oh never mind.) Unless you're truly gifted down there—and if you are, I applaud you—pants with an extra-long rise will only make you look like you're wearing Depends. I hate to see a guy with a really long rise, like when the pants are solid to his knees. Not a good look. But the converse of that is that your pants shouldn't be like a cheap hotel—no ball room. Got it? Good.

TIP

One of my general rules of shopping is that if you really want to know if it fits, unfortunately, you've got to try it on. But when it comes to the waist of your pants, there is a great shortcut I'll allow. If you're in a pinch, and you really don't want to try on a pair of pants, take them by the waist and wrap them around your neck. If they fit around your neck, they'll almost always fit your waist. Notice I said almost. Not foolproof, people.

Seat

The seat obviously refers to your tush, fanny, rump, or whatever cute pet name you choose to call it behind closed doors. The seat should fit so that you can tell you have a butt, yet stop short of being so tight that the pants accentuate your butt *crack*. An important distinction, people.

Okay, so now your pants will fit you. But what *kind* of pants do you need? Everyone needs khakis, corduroys, and jeans in their closet, so let's start there. Casual pants will be the bulk of your pants wardrobe.

CASUAL PANTS

Khaki: Friend or Foe?

Right now our great nation is in the midst of a raging khaki epidemic. Everyone and their brother thought that casual Friday meant they should go out and buy ninety pairs of Dockers. With all due respect to Dockers, guys need to mix it up a bit.

Sure, you should absolutely have some khakis, but make sure they're not pleated. My friend Lauren Weisberger says the devil wears Prada; I think the devil wears pleated khakis. There's nothing cleaner and crisper than a nice flat-front khaki pant, except maybe an extra-dry Ketel One martini. Khakis should always fit lean and mean, never baggy or bulky.

It's also important to remember that not all khaki is created equal. Most people don't realize there's a difference between fall and winter khaki and spring and summer khaki. Khaki for the colder seasons will come in a range of colors, from warm golden tones to browns, and will be a heavier weight. For spring and summer, your khakis should be lighter-weight cotton twill, and will come in a softer color palette—bone, sand, and putty tones. Summer khakis can even be almost white. I know—crazy, isn't it?

THE PANTS PYRAMID

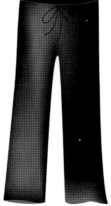

not for amateurs

drawstring pants

should have

cargo pants   *camp pants*

must have

khakis   *cords*   *jeans*

Corduroys

Corduroys are just a teensy bit dressier than khakis. Think of them as a cool alternative to jeans. Wear them for casual Fridays, with a sweater and an oxford shirt, or on a date, in place of denim. Much like denim, there are loads of different washes and finishes available. I recommend you have a pair of corduroys in a medium wale. I know that's a scary word, but wale just refers to the actual width of the "cord" in the corduroy. A super skinny wale will look a little bit dated, and a super wide wale can tend to make you look fat. And because I know you're going to ask: Yes, you can wear cords in summer.

Jeans, the American Dream

Jeans are an American icon, so we're going to spend a lot of time on them. And anytime you say icon, you have to think: "classic." There's so much out there in denim for you to choose from, it can get almost overwhelming. But you really shouldn't be getting mixed up with all that tricky novelty fashion denim. It's only going to get you into a lot of trouble, so proceed with caution. Sure, it can be fun to try something a little different, like a pair of designer jeans with a fun wash or pocket treatment, but stuff like that comes and goes like gypsies in the night. By the time you get home with the new style, it's already over. So why take the risk? Besides, we don't want to overdo your metrosexualization. If you are a straight man, there is absolutely no reason for you to be spending $285 on a pair of designer jeans when you can get a pair of good old traditional five-pocket, button-fly Levi's 501s instead for around $50. For most guys that's all you're ever really going to need.

Personally, I'm a big Levi's fan. Levi's are the Mercedes-Benz of denim. They invented the stuff and they know what they're doing. It's the real deal. Why mess with that? But Levi's don't work on everyone. Not to worry. There are many, many denim brands on the market; you just need to find the one that fits you best. So take a morning and try on all different kinds of jeans and see what works for you. Get a second opinion from your salesperson, or bring a friend—someone who'll tell you when you look fat, not phat. (You *want* to look phat, in case that wasn't clear.)

I don't want to get all Evita on you, dictating exactly what you should buy, but if

Here's a quick fix for one of life's eternal dilemmas: the proper length of your jeans. If you're a 31 waist and a 32 inseam, life is good. Just buy the size that fits you. But if you're a little bit chunkier, with a bigger waist and a shorter inseam, it can be hard to find jeans that fit you properly. I know it's traumatizing, but sometimes jeans that are big enough to fit you in the waist don't come in shorter lengths, so you have to buy a pair that's too long for you.

So then what do you do? The answer is *not* to cuff them, people, unless you want to look like a bad James Dean impersonator or Potsie from *Happy Days*. What you want to do is take your jeans to your friendly neighborhood tailor, have them cut to the proper length, and then have the original bottom hem reattached. The bottom hem will have the original stitching, and will have wear and tear engineered into it. If you just hem the pants without putting the bottom hem back on, the bottoms of your jeans will look perfectly clean and unabraded. That's a little too *Leave It to Beaver*.

you're going to have only one pair of jeans, I think a good choice is a classic Levi's 501 in the medium indigo wash. And then if you wear lots of denim, you can also have a dark wash pair, which tends to look a little dressier, and maybe a pair of white denim for summer. I don't like any of those fancy washes, like the ones that make you look like you just sat in wet paint or like someone just sandblasted your ass. And black denim? Nuh-uh. Best left for fashion-forward clergy and Shakira, unkay?

I also love vintage denim, which should always be in your wardrobe. You can spend thousands of dollars on it at a fancy vintage store, or you check out your local secondhand store. You can also buy new denim jeans that have been washed in certain enzymes and treated so that they're broken in and feel like a comfortable pair you've had for a lifetime. Jeans should have personality.

In terms of fit, jeans are by nature a little less smart and correct than other types of pants. They don't have to fit tightly like dress pants. I love when jeans look more relaxed, slouchy, and a little blown out.

CARSON K.
JEANS COMPANY

RING SPUN DENIM
MEDIUM INDIGO COLOR
4 BUTTON FLY
STRAIGHT LEG

31 X 34

Jeans are sometimes sized very randomly. So just because you're one size in one brand, you're not necessarily going to be the same size in another. Some manufacturers even add an inch or two to the waist-band, just to make it even trickier. They say it's a 30, but if you measure, it's really more like a 32. It's a marketing ploy to make you feel better. Then you buy the jeans because you say, "Oh my God! It's a 30 and it fits! I'll take ten pairs!" Nice try, world denim cartel!

Hopefully, in an ideal world, everybody's waist size is smaller than the length. When you get to be a 38/31, it's just a sad scenario, Humpty Dumpty. Buy the length closest to your real length. If that means you have to measure your inseam with a tape measure, that's fine. Just do it. It's fun working down there. Measure from the inside of the crotch, where the rise seam ends, to the bottom hem. And whatever you measure, that's probably your size, because most denim is already preshrunk. All this "shrink to fit" stuff is crap. If they fit your body in the store, odds are they will fit correctly after washing.

The wash refers to the color and fade of the jeans, which can be anywhere from a really uniform, super dark midnight blue to a soft light blue with lots of streaks and variations. In order to achieve a lot of those looks, denim is often treated; it's thrown in big industrial washing machines, either with special enzymes or pumice stones to break down the fabric and give it a softer, more lived-in patina. Or sometimes jeans are actually sandblasted. There are a million and one processes used in denim, and that's why it's best to keep it simple. When in doubt, think, "What would Carson do?" The answer: You're always better off with simple and classic.

Boot-leg (or boot cut) jeans were made for cow-boys, and that's why they're cut the way they are. Boot legs have very slim lines so they won't bunch up in the saddle or cause lumps at the knees when riding. They will also have a slight flare to accom-modate cowboy boots. Boot leg is also the one cut that's pretty consistent from brand to brand. If it's called boot leg, you can be pretty sure it's going to be leaner through the seat and thighs, with a slightly flared bottom.

Relaxed or easy fit No two designers will call this the same thing, but I like to call it the "Oh my God, Becky! Her butt is so big" fit. The waist and the length are still the same, but the space between them, the whole construction of the jean, is more generous in the seat, thigh, and leg.

Straight leg No pun intended. These are not only for straight men, as you may have thought. It's just a little bit of a leaner cut—there's no flare like in a boot cut. They just basically cut a big square out for your leg. Straight-leg jeans work for just about everyone. I don't ever want to see denim that's pegged. That worked in the eighties, when you tight rolled the hem of your jeans and cuffed it three times to wear with your Coca-Cola rugby shirt, Reeboks, and Swatch watch. It might still be all the rage in Uzbekistan, but not so much here anymore.

What Should a Good Pair of Jeans Do for You?

1 They should fit and flatter.

2 They should feel like you've worn them forever.

3 They should make you feel at your most comfortable.

4 They should give you a nice basket, even if it's not Easter.

5 They should make you look and feel sexy.

6 They should go with just about everything else in your wardrobe.

7 They should get you laid. Oh, come on. Stop pretending to be shocked.

The flasher might say "low rise" or "medium rise." Let's hope they never make a high rise. I recommend medium rise. We don't want to see your happy trail. As sexy as it may have looked in the International Male catalog, trust me, it's not a good look for you. And don't get me started on the other side, where we see ass crack. There's a reason Whitney said, "Crack is whack." Crack kills, people, and it will kill your look.

A WORD OF CAUTION: Low-slung jeans worn gangsta style make you look like you have a load in your pants. Let's leave that to our friends in the rap community, shall we? How do you know if you've gone too low? Well, if you can see your underwear or your pubic hair (and your name is not Britney or Christina), your low riders are too low. If the end of your fly zipper is at your knees, that's also a good sign your jeans are too loose. That's okay for the artist formerly known as Lil' Bow Wow, but not for you.

Roughwear Pants

Despite your dirty fantasies, roughwear pants are just more rugged, outdoorsy pants for weekend wear. They include things like cargo pants and painters' pants—anything with a utility or workwear heritage. They pay homage to the blue-collar laborer who made this land of ours so great. And they look as hot today as they did when the WPA was introduced. Thank you, President Roosevelt! Roughwear pants are rugged, they're meant to take a licking, and there are so many options out there. One pair of pants I love, although they're no longer readily available, are the Alcatraz pants by G-Star, which are prison-inspired and super cool. Totally hot in an *Oz* kind of way.

Roughwear pants are generally reserved for outdoor activities like football games, weekend projects, trips to the Home Depot, and the gay rugby national championships. They're meant to be worn with a rugged boot or a bulky fisherman sweater or a barn jacket. They're mostly for winter wear. Who wants to be running around in cargo pants in the heat of the summer?

A WORD ABOUT CARGO PANTS: Cargo pants are a fun fashion statement that have pretty much become a staple. I think they're here to stay, so you can feel pretty safe buying a pair. (I had a phase where I wore leather cargos and looked like I worked at Old Navy Germany. But ich digress.)

I know there is at least one suburban dad somewhere reading this who's thinking that cargo pants are way too "out there" for him. You have to get beyond that. I'm here for you. Cargos can add a sense of youthfulness to your look—as long as they fit well and don't have too many pockets. I would caution everyone to use them

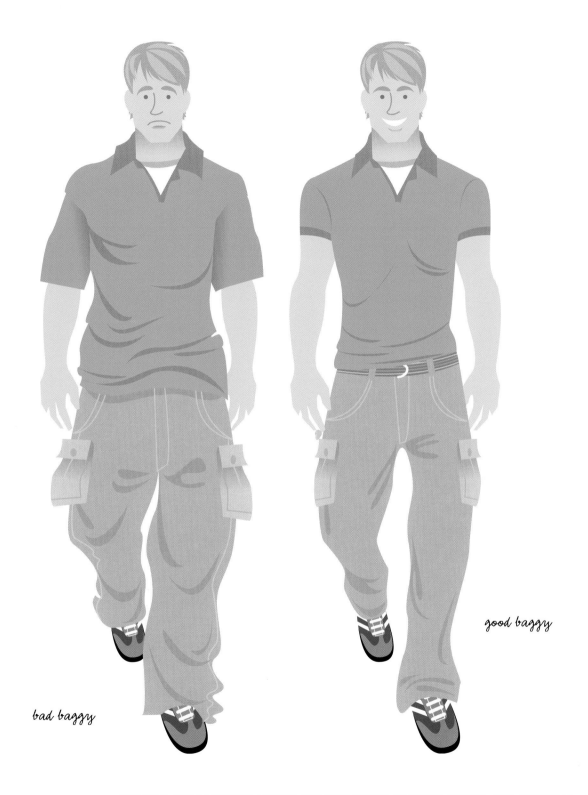

bad baggy

good baggy

sparingly, though. If you can move the entire contents of your home or apartment just by putting things in your cargo pants, they probably have too many pockets. We have homes. We have offices. We don't need to load our cargos up with all of our life's possessions. If you don't have a home or an office, at least rent a locker at the airport or your local bowling alley. They're cargo pants, they're not a storage unit.

Drawstring Pants

These are great for summer, the beach, and vacations. A pair of drawstring pants with a white T-shirt and flip-flops is a wonderful, easy breezy, relaxed kind of look, but drawstring pants probably don't fill a need other than that. They're sketchy because they're a little too close to elastic waistband pants, which are always the wrong answer. They can make you look like you're wearing pajamas in the middle of the day, which just screams elder care facility, or homelessness, or institutionalization. Not cute. So be careful.

DRESS PANTS

Although most of America has gone casual, some people still need to get dressed up, either for work or for other settings like dates or nights on the town. Which brings us to the wide world of dress pants or "slacks," as a lot of old ladies like to call them. (They're the same ones who call women's shirts "blouses.") Here we're basically talking anything that's not khaki, cord, or denim.

Summer dress pants can be made of linen, lightweight cotton twill, poplin, or seersucker (I love saying that word!), while winter ones might be wool, heavyweight cotton twill, suede, leather, or yes, my favorite, cashmere blend.

The great thing about dress pants is you can add a variety of sport coats, sweaters, and patterned shirts to top them off. These will give you tremendous versatility. And you know how we love versatility in the gay community!

Generally, you'll get more bang for your buck if you buy a couple pairs of solid-colored, well-fitting dress pants. No pleats, please. If you have a pair in gray flannel, a pair in black or navy wool, and you throw in a herringbone or tweed pant, you'll have

One of my favorite clothing myths is the idea that wearing baggy clothes will make you look thinner. It will not. You will just look like you have size dyslexia. People will not think you have miraculously slimmed down; they'll just think you're an idiot. Or wonder, "Hmmm. Why is George wearing those humongous pants that don't fit him?" Clothing can help change your overall look, but it's not meant to perform magic tricks. That's for David Copperfield and his fine colleagues. A simple rule of thumb is that you should wear clothing that fits the day that you're planning to wear it. Don't wear clothing that you'll grow into, you'll lose weight for, etc. Let's live for the moment, people! Carpe diem!

the ammo to pair them up with interesting shirts and sweaters and make lots of interesting looks. For summer, lighten the color palette to include sand, white, and classic navy.

Don't forget the proper accoutrements. It's important that you have dress shoes, a dress belt, and a beautiful shirt to go with your dress pants. Sneakers with dress pants and a T-shirt is a cute look for Ashton Kutcher (a former model) or me (a stylist), but it's definitely not for amateurs. It will inevitably make you look like you're on your way to the typing pool at IBM. Do they even have typing pools anymore? Discuss.

By the way, dress socks go with dress shoes that go with dress pants. They shouldn't be athletic socks or tube socks. And they shouldn't be women's hosiery. Yikes!

SHORTS

Just like for pants, it's a jungle out there as far as shorts are concerned. But to make it easier on you, my rules for shorts are pretty much the same as my rules for pants: Avoid pleats, and make sure they fit, which includes the fit of the rise and the seat. Stay away from elastic waistbands and drawstrings.

To me, shorts are really for weekends and vacations—not for the office. They were conceived for casual country club or beachside living, which is important to remember when you pair them with shoes. Shorts are meant to be worn with a classic tennis shoe, a sandal, flip-flop, driving moc, loafer, or boat shoe. Wearing any other kind of lace-up shoes with shorts is always the wrong answer. The only people who pull it off are the postal workers. And we all know how edgy they are! I also want you to be wary of the shorts, socks, and Birkenstocks look, which inevitably makes you look like a German tourist or a *High Times* subscriber. If you walk up to a stranger, they'll think you're asking for directions to I-95 or to a Phish concert.

The final stop on our covering-your-ass journey:

SWIMWEAR

Unfortunately, there always seems to be an inverse relationship between how obese or overweight some men are and the size of their swimwear. Meaning that the bigger they are, the smaller their swimwear. Not a good idea. For just about all men, I recommend a swim trunk that comes to mid-thigh. Avoid the clam digger or anything that even approaches the clam digger, because anything that's too long will make your legs look short and stumpy. Avoid any bodyhugging spandex. And for God's sake, avoid thongs, aka the banana hammock. I don't want to see your moons over Miami.

Your swim trunks should be made out of a quick dry nylon with a *fixed* waistband. There's a misconception that an elastic waistband on a swimsuit will make you look slimmer. But the elastic waistband is just the pleated pants of swimwear. They'll only accentuate your waistline. But if your waistband is fixed, that means you need to make sure the trunks actually fit you. Trust me, they'll be much more flattering than looking like you have a gathered garbage bag around your waist or you're wearing a diaper. The Huggies look is so rarely the right answer on a grown man.

Most straight men are afraid of the bikini, as they well should be. But every once in a while you get some jackass who thinks he looks hot in a bikini. And that could ruin a day at the beach for everyone. (And you thought *Jaws* made you afraid of going in the water!) Unless you're a member of the Olympic water polo team, you own a house on Fire Island, or you're a hot Brazilian man named Sergio, the bikini should be avoided at all costs.

Always the Wrong Answer . . .

Overalls. Not unless they're bringing back Hee Haw. I love the sight of a man in a hardhat, all dressed up in blue-collar regalia, building bridges across the waterways of the Midwest. But it's not a fashion statement.

pleated pants. Do I have to say anything more?

Track pants. Nylon track pants for the gym are fine. But you should never wear the whole track suit. It brings back many bad airport memories. Store them in two different parts of the house.

Acid-washed jeans. Unless you're going to the MC Hammer reunion tour.

Sarongs. I don't think so. Sound it out. So wrong.

PREPPY CHIC

Chest Wear That's Best Wear

SHIRTS AND SWEATERS, BABY

SO NOW THAT WE'VE TALKED ABOUT BOTTOMS, IT'S TIME TO TALK ABOUT ANYTHING THAT GOES ON TOP. GET YOUR MIND OUT OF THE gutter, people! I mean shirts and sweaters.

SHIRTS

Let's start out with that old standby, the sport shirt. I bet you've been lying awake at night wondering, "Carson, just what is a sport shirt?" Well, a sport shirt is any kind of long- or short-sleeve woven shirt with buttons that isn't a dress shirt—it can be a linen shirt, a cotton oxford, or a dressier novelty shirt. It can sport stripes or bear gingham, paisley, whatever. Now, I know a lot of you have cotton oxfords and long-sleeve, woven button-down shirts and you think they're dress shirts. Well, they're not.

How can you tell the difference? Dress shirts will be more tailored so that they fit under a suit. They'll also be better constructed and have more intricate detailing. Dress shirts are also made of a finer gauge of cotton. The gauge of a fiber is just like the gauge of a train track, or a shotgun. (Like I would know!) The finer the gauge, that is, the skinnier and more delicate the fiber, the dressier the shirts will look. It's just like the thread count of sheets. The really, really fine expensive sheets with a high thread count are soft and smooth, and the less expensive, lower quality ones are a little more rugged. But there's a downside to high-quality cotton. Since it's more delicate, it won't wear as well or last as long.

Ever since America went casual and so many men stopped wearing ties regularly, the sport shirt has become the item with which men can make a fashion statement. That's why you see a lot of people wearing striped sport shirts with jeans and loafers. I think that's a perfect date outfit. Throw on a blazer and you're golden, pony boy. Now, I love that look, but that doesn't mean you should overdo it. You shouldn't have eighty striped shirts in your closet just because that's the current trend. I say get yourself a couple and ride the wave.

A general rule of thumb to avoid getting into trouble with your sport shirts is to make sure they're 100 percent cotton. Two words that freak me out are "wrinkle free." It's like Olestra. There's something about it that's just not right. Cotton with stretch? Cotton-polyester blends? Not so much. Either your shirts are cotton or they're not. It's like being a little bit gay, and we all know you can't be just a little bit gay.

It's really important to wear sport shirts that fit. Because of our addiction to fast food, many sport shirts are made oversized. I beg you to get the correct size. Your shirt should be loose enough that you can move around comfortably. It shouldn't be binding or super narrow. On the other hand, if you've been busy blasting your delts at the gym (yum!), a shirt might fit you in the shoulders yet be huge and boxy everywhere else. Sturdy and boxy is good when it comes to a Volvo to transport your baby niece Kimber, because that's precious cargo, but you don't want your sport shirts to fit like a Volvo. For just five or ten dollars, you can visit your friendly neighborhood tailor and have the shirt taken in on the side seam. You'll look more fit immediately, without even a visit to that pesky gym.

This brings us to another important point: Make sure you try on when shopping. People think a shirt is a shirt is a shirt. It's not. Each designer or manufacturer sizes their shirts differently. If you really can't bear to get naked in a public dressing room—no, there aren't cameras in there, get over your *Sliver* fantasy—it's perfectly acceptable to buy it, take it home, and try it on in the comfort of your own home. Then if it doesn't fit, you can make a day to go back and return it. CAUTION: This

"MAKES YOU GAY…"

I've said before that I love nothing more than a crisp pink oxford. There appears to be a misconception among my straight brethren that a straight man shouldn't wear pink shirts because wearing pink makes you gay. I have an important news fuh-lash for you.

Wearing pink doesn't make you gay.

Getting a little too "excited" during *Wrestlemania*, on the other hand, does make you gay.

So this got me thinking that I could provide similar helpful advice to separate the fauxmosexuals—so much better than metrosexual, don't you think? Metrosexual sounds like people having sex on the bus!—from the real men.

DOESN'T MAKE
YOU GAY

DOESN'T MAKE YOU GAY	MAKES YOU GAY
Moisturizing	Taking an all-male cruise to Latin America
Using "product" on your hair	Wearing wigs
Getting highlights in your hair	Giving other people highlights
Getting manicures	Getting *French* manicures
Waxing your eyebrows	Plucking them to "open up your eye"
Having facial hair	Sporting a mustache, circa 1979 *Magnum P.I.*

requires two trips to the mall. And as we all know, fossil fuels are dwindling. So why not just try it on when you're at the store? You do the math.

Now we get to the actual content of your sport shirt repertoire. One sport shirt you should absolutely have in your closet is an oxford shirt, which can work with everything from a pair of jeans to a blue blazer. I'm going to hope that you already know what an oxford shirt is: a sturdy, heavier-weight pinpoint cotton weave with little buttons on the collar. The oxford shirt originated in Britain and is the backbone of British style—what we think of as classic English dressing. It came to America through prep schools and Brooks Brothers, bless their blue-blooded little hearts. If everyone in America owned a pink oxford, the world would be a much better place.

Everyone should also have at least one or two linen shirts in their wardrobe. They're so classic and good-looking. For the fashion impaired among you, linen is a nubbly, textured lightweight fabric made from flax. Just make sure your linen shirts are hefty enough so we don't see your nipples or your chest hair. I might like that, but let's spare the rest of America, shall we?

Linen will wrinkle like crazy, but it's meant to, so deal with it. I do recommend linen shirts more than linen pants, because sitting in pants you can really get some crazy wrinkles, like cat whiskers on the crotch. But that's why linen is only meant for casual settings. It's better to be all wrinkled when you're at the beach having a margarita than when you're applying to refinance your mortgage.

The other important thing to remember about linen is that you need to wear it between Memorial Day and Labor Day. Wearing linen when it's ten degrees out only makes you look like you have seasonal dyslexia. It's like, "Hi, how long have you had amnesia? You live in Minneapolis, not Maui." The only exception to this rule is for our friends in California and Florida, where you can luxuriate in linen year round. Oh, happy day!

I also love printed novelty shirts and think everyone should have some. Go ahead, have fun, but keep the prints subtle. Your penchant for Hello Kitty does not need to be shared with the world via your clothing. Printed Hawaiian shirts have gotten so popular that I see guys wearing them everywhere. Casual Friday does not equal Hawaiian shirts, kids. They're meant for vacations and barbecues, not annual

Sport Shirts with French Cuffs

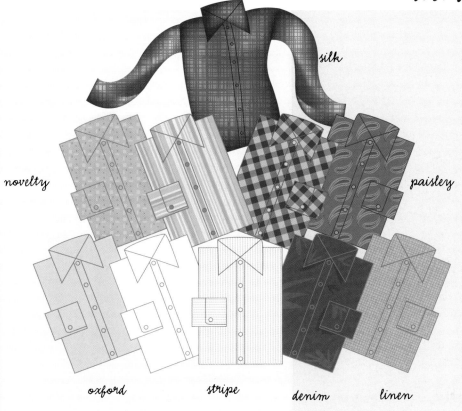

silk

novelty

paisley

oxford

stripe

denim

linen

These days, there are a lot of sport shirts out there with French cuffs. It's a fashion thing. They're wonderful, and it can be a great look. You can either invest in an inexpensive pair of cuff links (see chapter seven for more), or if you want to go for a more casual look, you can just tszuj the sleeves up and forget the cuff links. But the important lesson here, friends, is don't be afraid of French cuffs. French tourists are another matter completely.

stockholder meetings. I don't want to see the CEO of the International Edible Underwear Council giving a speech on the state of the industry when he looks like he works as a host at Trader Vic's. Don't get me wrong, I loved *Fantasy Island*, just not so much the fashion.

You'll notice that in our grand tour of the wide world of sport shirts I didn't mention flannel, much to the chagrin of our lesbian friends. I know you already have some flannel in your closet, so just promise me you'll wear it sparingly. It's just too Paul Bunyan for most guys, so step away from the flannel, people.

I'm also not a big fan of men in silk shirts. It's hard for guys to pull it off. Most guys wearing a silk shirt look like they're waiting for the valet to bring their IROC-Z, they're in their pajamas, or they're waiting for the next Air India flight to Bombay.

SHIlishing

DRESS SHIRTS

Dress shirts are the more expensive shirts you'd wear with a suit and a tie. They should be 100 percent cotton, and will be made of a dressier, smoother, more luxurious cotton than your sport shirts, since they're meant for dressier occasions.

If you don't wear a suit to the office every day, odds are you're not going to need that many dress shirts. Since they're expensive, there's no need to make that investment. I'd rather see you take your money and buy a cool sport shirt or a cashmere sweater. All the average guy needs is a few really great dress shirts, so get yourself a white one, a blue one, and maybe a stripe, and you'll be fine. Invest in quality rather than quantity.

Dress shirts are meant to fit precisely, so it's important to pay attention to sizing. If you're in doubt about your size, go to a fine quality department store or menswear store and have them measure you. A lot of people haven't been measured since they got out of high school, and they still think they're the same size. I have news for you: You're probably not.

The first thing to consider is sleeve length. When you have your suit jacket on, you want to see about one quarter inch of the shirt cuff. The cuffs should fall roughly one inch below your wrist bone. If your mom smoked during pregnancy, your arms may be longer than usual. You just have to be vigilant about getting the right size—they're out there, I promise.

Dress shirts are also going to fit differently in the neck from sport shirts. When you button the neck on a sport shirt, it's not going to be an authentic fit. It will be sized bigger than your neck, because it's meant to be worn open, not all buttoned up, like Miss Beadle on *Little House on the Prairie*. Dress shirts, on the other hand, are true to fit. When you button them closed to wear a tie—which is what they're meant for, people—they should fit your neck snugly. That means you should be able to easily

As long as your dress shirts are 100 percent cotton, they're good quality, and they fit you, I don't care where you buy them. You can get great quality dress shirts from well-known designers at stores like Marshalls and T.J.Maxx for about $19. They'll definitely have the basics there, although it might require a little digging. If you're not up for that, you'll probably find the best selection and variety at a department store. They'll also have the best selection of ties and will have a friendly sales professional who can help you select shirts and mix and match them with your ties.

slide two fingers inside the collar: no more, no less. If you find yourself wanting to make the international choking sign, that's not a good fit.

Now, I don't want to confuse you, but you need to know that most dress shirts are made of fine cotton that is not preshrunk like sportswear is. So when you try them on for the first time, the neck may be a teeny bit large, and the sleeves may be a little long. That's okay. After about three washings, they'll shrink to the right size. You'll also find that dress shirts might be leaner in the side seams, so they're not bulky under your suit jacket. And the shirttail may be longer than a sport shirt, so it stays tucked in to your pants.

A lot of men seem completely lost when it comes to choosing the right kind of collar. That's okay, that's why you have me. Collars are important because your face is your art, and your collar frames your face and draws the eye upward. Find the collar type that looks best on you, and don't worry about all those rules you've read in men's magazines that say things like "If you have a long, round face, you can only wear this kind of collar." If you have a long, round face, you need surgery. Just kidding, people. But don't worry that there's only one kind of collar that you can wear with your short, fat head. Everyone's different. There is no absolute rule, except that you should keep it in balance.

Now, just because you find you like the look of, say, a tab collar, you still need to have a good mix. Aside from point collars, which are very versatile and can basically be worn with everything, your collar choice should go back to the dressiness of what you're wearing with it. A spread collar, for example, is more of a dressy, suit look. The oxford button-down is more relaxed, and looks great with a blue blazer or a tweed jacket—or open with a great pair of pecs!

Point collar. Dressier than a button-down, the point collar is the most common and versatile. You can wear it open without a tie if you want to, or pair it with a sweater or a suit. It's the switch-hitter of dress shirts. God, I love using sports lingo.

Spread collar. Calm down. Not that kind of spread. This is one you really have to wear with a tie. Because it's a spread collar, without a tie there would be a big gap in the middle. And you would look like a nun. Never the right answer, people.

Tab collar. That little bridge of cotton that holds the collar in place behind your tie makes for a very, very neat and conservative, dressed-up, and well-tailored look, meant to go with a dressier suit. Yes, you have to wear a tie with this one.

White contrast collar. This is where the body of the shirt is a color, but the collar is white. This is a very dressed-up, very English look. It's really, really sharp—just think of Robert Redford in *The Great Gatsby*. Sigh. Maybe that doesn't make you as happy as it makes me.

SHIRTS

DRESS

Polo-style knit shirts are comfortable classic standbys. If you have five of these in your closet—a black one, a white one, and a few fun colors, in a mix of short and long sleeves—you'll never go wrong. This shirt is one of the most versatile pieces of clothing in your wardrobe. Everyone looks great in a polo, and it always has a certain preppy chic sophistication that works for most occasions as well as the casual work environment. Pair it with denim, wear it to work with khakis and a blazer, or throw one on with shorts at the beach, and you'll always look cool. I wouldn't wear one to a wedding, but to a casual dinner in the Hamptons? Absotively!

The polo shirt is not to be confused with the Polo shirt, as in the Ralph Lauren brand. It's just any short-sleeve knit shirt in a style that was originally used for playing polo.

I bet you're waiting for me to give the step-by-step on how to iron a shirt. Surprise! I'm not. Because unless you live in Cambodia, there is no reason for not sending your dress shirts to the cleaners. It costs a dollar, people. And if you can't come up with that dollar, you have bigger issues than wrinkly shirts.

As for how much starch to use, it's a very personal preference. When you heavily starch a shirt, it feels like you're wearing cardboard. That's a great way to get a full body dermabrasion without seeing a dermatologist, but I really can't recommend it. Heavy starch only magnifies and intensifies wrinkling, because it makes the shirt too crisp and hard. The moment you sit, those wrinkles are also going to be permanently etched into your shirt. So follow your hearts, but if you're committed to heavy starch, promise me you'll at least give light starch a try. And maybe then you'll see the light.

It's that heritage that makes the shirt comfortable, breathable, cool, sexy, and sophisticated. Just look at where it came from, and you'll see why it's so cool. While the design of the polo shirt was perfected by Lacoste and Ralph Lauren, your knit shirts don't have to have a logo. It's really a matter of personal preference. I don't care if you're sporting the Polo pony, the Lacoste crocodile, Le Tigre, or Bozo the Clown. (Okay, maybe not so much Bozo the Clown.) As long as it fits and it looks good, it doesn't matter where it's from.

Now, a lot of people think that a polo shirt and a golf shirt are the same. They're not. The golf shirt looks like the polo shirt and is similarly constructed, but it's a very different animal, *mon frère*. The polo shirt is meant to be a little more tailored and sophisticated. I know this might come as a shock, but a golf shirt is meant for playing golf. It has a very specific function and fit, like roominess in the shoulders and waist to allow for lots of twisting in the torso. The sleeve goes to the elbow, because if you were wearing a regular polo shirt while teeing off, a lot of your arm would show. And that might not be so much fun for your fellow players. Personally, I don't golf, but I like to dress up and *pretend* I'm golfing, just so I can wear the clothes. As long as the clothes are cute, keep swinging away, people!

The knit shirt is also an area where the straight guy should be cautious and not fall victim to the lure of the free shirt. Why? Well, there's a reason they're free. You get what you pay for, silly!

Bad = oversized golf shirt, pleated Dockers, holding a Bud in a beer cozy

good = polo shirt, jeans, blue blazer, fun belt, tennis shoes

GOLF BARN

A lot of companies give out free knit shirts with corporate logos. Bad idea. You don't want to look like you're renting shoes at a bowling alley or driving the tram to the Tinkerbell Lot at Disney World. Unless you are. And there's no shame in that, kids.

While it pains me greatly, I realize that some of you may have to wear these logoed knit shirts at the annual trade show or as part of your daily uniform. But don't let me catch you in them Friday after five. Like a hooker after sunup, those things better go into hiding.

T-SHIRTS

There's nothing sexier than a clean, nicely broken-in, cuddly white cotton crewneck T-shirt worn with jeans, a charismatic belt, and some loafers. I think that's hot. You're done. It's so very James Dean. If you buy some well-fitted, high-quality T-shirts to wear alone or layer under other things—three in white, three in black, and three in heathered gray—that's the most bang for $7.50 a pop that you'll ever have, unless there's a trip to Thailand in your future.

Just like most things, I don't really care where you buy them. The Gap is fine. Old Navy is fine. As long as it's hefty, nice cotton with a well-constructed ribbed collar, it's going to look great. But once again, I'm not talking about underwear T-shirts that are sheer enough to show your nipples. Wrong answer. (See chapter two on underwear.)

You might also want to season your wardrobe—pepper it, if it you will—with a few novelty shirts. There's been a big vintage T-shirt craze that's swept our great nation. They're available everywhere. But what made the vintage ones great was the quirkiness of their design, the logos, the color schemes, or the quizzical commercial mottoes. When those great old designs are knocked off and reproduced en masse by major corporate retailers, they lose their panache. When every guy on the street has the same faux vintage Larry's Lube Stop tee that he bought at the mall for $18.99, it's no longer hip. So why get an imposter when you can have the real thing? A quick visit to the local Goodwill or to a more upscale thrift store, and you can find great, broken-in, soft, cuddly vintage tees for pennies on the dollar of what you'd pay at a "full retail" store. And they're authentic, which is the key word. A good rule of thumb, by the way, is to avoid any clothing that actually says the word "authentic" on it.

SWEATERS

Sweaters are an important part of any guy's wardrobe. A few sweaters will really go a long way, especially if you invest in flattering colors. (Hint: Taupey, flesh-toned colors just don't look good on anyone. Matching your clothes to your skin tone is a really bad idea.) A fine-gauge sweater is a great way to look dressed up without wearing a woven shirt or a sport coat. It's perfect for dates.

You should definitely have a few crewneck sweaters. The crewneck is versatile because it can look fantastic with a T-shirt or a dress shirt underneath, although I prefer a T-shirt. You should also have one or two V-neck sweaters. They're a bit harder to wear and tend to look a little guidofied, so it is crucial that they be worn with a woven shirt with a collar. A T-shirt under a V-neck is a no-no.

If you're feeling a little frisky, you might want to throw a cardigan or a zip-up sweater into the mix. The cardigan is not just for Fred Rogers anymore, and can actually be very chic. The important thing here is fit, fit, fit. An ill-fitting cardigan is the first step to homelessness.

Last but not least, man's best friend. No, not your right hand or your golden retriever, but the trusty turtleneck. Every man should own at least one black turtleneck. They are chic, slim, and versatile like me!

Sweaters are all about the fiber of which they are constructed. When you buy a sweater, you should really consider the climate in which you live and how much use you're going to get out of it. There's no color-coded fiber chart of the U.S., like they have for flower bulbs, but I think you can figure it out. If you live in Hawaii, you're not going to get much use out of those bulky fisherman knits, and linen rollnecks won't be that helpful during Michigan winters.

Guys know what cotton and polyester are, but you don't know yarns, so here's a little cheat sheet.

too cold: relocate

wool, merino, linen, and cashmere

merino, cotton, linen, and cashmere

cotton, linen, and cashmere

Fiber Map of the U.S.A.

Cashmere

What's all the fuss about cashmere? It's as expensive as cosmetic surgery. Wait, let me think of a good straight guy analogy. Cashmere is the flat-screen TV of yarns. It's the Super Bowl of sweaters.

Cashmere comes from a goat, imagine that. Specifically, it's from the soft belly hair of a goat from the Kashmir region of India. It's expensive because it takes forever for our goat friends to grow enough hair to make one sweater. It's a luxury because it's super warm and cuddly. Cashmere is cute cubed—cute, cute, cute!

But alas, all cashmere is not created equal. Just like beef, where you have prime, choice, and grade A, there are different quality levels of fibers. Some manufacturers use a very low-grade cashmere, so you really have to feel the quality and comparison shop a little. It's all right, cop a good feel. This is one place where you won't get sued if you touch.

How to Make Friends with Cashmere

Ordinarily, a decent cashmere sweater will run you between $150 and $400. I don't want you to have to take out a second mortgage to afford one, so here's a useful tip. Head to a department store in the few days after Christmas. You can often still find a very good selection at deeply reduced prices—often as much as 50 percent off. And once you bring your little cashmere friend home, don't neglect its needs. You might think it best to send your cashmere to a professional dry cleaner, but you need to resist that urge. Dry-cleaning strips cashmere of the essential natural oils that make it so soft and cuddly. Just wash it yourself with a capful of Woolite and lay it flat to dry.

Merino

This is the poor man's cashmere, a very popular and less costly alternative. Merino is actually a very high-quality, luxurious wool that comes from the merino sheep of New Zealand. They're a little bit dressier than other wool sweaters, they're a little bit cooler, and a nice alternative to the more expensive fibers. Think of your merino sweaters as baby steps on the glorious road to cashmere.

Lambswool

Lambswool falls in the same category as merino—it's more lightweight than regular wool and generally a little finer quality and more dressed up. Because it comes from baby sheep, the fibers are younger and softer.

Wool

You probably already know that wool comes from our little sheep friends. Natural fibers are always better because when woven into a sweater, they do exactly what the fiber was intended to do in nature: keep the animal warm and wick away moisture. And they'll do the same for you, tiger.

When you take care of your wool sweaters, remember the wool was once a living thing. So when you're storing it, it needs room to breathe. It can't be suffocated or overheated, and needs to be cared for properly. It's kind of like your hair, which is essentially dead on the top of your head, but it's still an organic material. Of course, some of us have hair that is more dead than others'. And you know who you are.

Cotton

Cotton sweaters are great, especially for those gentle readers who live in warmer states like Texas, California, and Florida. They're a good alternative because they provide warmth but are not super, super warm like cashmere or wool.

The care and laundering of cotton sweaters can be a bit tricky. Because they're cotton, they have a lot of flex to the fiber and can stretch out very easily. Much like it's effect on your mother's breasts, gravity is not your cotton sweaters' friend. Before you know it, you have a full-blown Jennifer-Beals-in-*Flashdance* look going. This is very easy to avoid, people. If you have a shoulder showing, or have the urge to cinch your cotton sweater with a belt and wear it with leg warmers and tap shoes, it's time to get rid of it.

I divide my sweaters into two categories: city and country. City sweaters are lean and mean, and country sweaters are big and chunky. The first rule of thumb is that your top and bottom halves need to match. If you're wearing a big, chunky, rugged fisherman knit sweater, your bottom needs to be rugged, too. Unlike your favorite bisexual, your country sweater doesn't go both ways. Don't wear a big fisherman's sweater with a beautiful silk-and-wool suit pant. Instead, wear it with something as casual as cargos or jeans, or dress it up with a Harris tweed blazer.

You'll also want to remember that super chunky ski sweaters and really thick fisherman knit sweaters were designed with a purpose: to keep you super warm outdoors. Keep in mind that in today's climate-controlled world, if you're going to be indoors, at work, shopping, or wherever, you're probably going to be too warm in one of them. They tend to be expensive because they use a lot of yarn, so invest in only one or

Your Shirts: When to Say Good-bye

- If it's stained

- If you can see your elbows

- If the collar is as yellow as the "before" pictures of dentures in those Efferdent commercials

- Pitted-out shirts are just plain grody! If you haven't been able to Shout it out, throw it out.

The Sweatshirt and Sports Jersey: Proceed with Caution!

Sweatshirts are only for the gym, people. Anything with the word "sweat" in it should not be part of your regular wardrobe. I don't mind a classic collegiate sweatshirt or a classic Champion to work out in, but not to wear out to dinner. The only exception is the vintage sweatshirt, which can be fun. What I really hate are the gigantic oversized sweatshirts that say "Minnesota Golden Gophers" or some other slogan. People in sweatshirts just look sloppy, like they should be at home painting their bathroom.

Let's be clear about something: Sports jerseys are a uniform. Period. If you're actually a professional athlete, or you're the guy who drives the Zamboni, they're okay; if you're watching in the stands, you're not fooling anyone. We know you're not Wayne Gretzky. A jersey should *never* be worn on a date, unless it's a same-sex date with a member of the opposing hockey team. The best thing you could do with team jerseys is take some advice from the Hard Rock Cafe and frame them. They'll be just the thing for the walls of your basement rec room.

Good: **Lean-fitting vintage sweatshirt with a shirt and tie under it and some chinos**

Bad: **Baggy sweatshirt, baggy pants, trucker cap**

two, because you won't have that much occasion to wear them unless you live in Maine. Otherwise, these sweaters are best left for skiing and outdoor activity, perhaps some apple picking on a brisk November morning.

Always the Wrong Answer . . .

Short-sleeve dress shirts. Please!

Pocket protectors. Never.

Mock turtles. The mock neck is called such because people mock you when you wear one. Any slinky silk mock-neck tees should be avoided at all costs; you'll look like an eighties porn star.

Novelty sweaters. Turkeys, Christmas trees, football logos, and fire trucks are all wrong, wrong, wrong. The one exception is the snowflake and reindeer sweater, which might be just too cute to pass up. All others are left for grandmas, babies, and preschool teachers.

A shirt and tie with no jacket. If you go that far, you should go all the way. Otherwise you look like an IRS employee. Note to IRS employees: Put on a jacket with that tie!

Fashion tees with logos. When your shirt features a giant designer logo, you risk looking like a walking billboard.

Everyone Looks Good in a Suit, Period

SUITS, BLAZERS, TIES, AND POCKET SQUARES

SUITS

There are two kinds of guys: Guys who wear suits every day, and those who wear them to weddings and funerals. No matter which kind of guy you are, and whether you have ten suits in your closet or just one, your suits should all be fantastic. Nothing makes you feel as good, important, and powerful; and nothing makes a guy look more handsome than a good suit. Just look at Donald Trump, from the forehead down. And nothing makes a guy look more pathetic than a bad suit.

As much as we've become a casual society, I still believe that every man absolutely needs to have a suit in his closet. Not everyone goes to fancy coming-out cotillions and needs a tuxedo (shocker, I know), and not every man wears a suit to work every day anymore. But weddings, funerals, and divorce court are just part of our lives, people. And for those occasions, you're going to have to buy a suit.

The great thing about suits is that they hardly ever change. If you buy a good quality suit with a classic silhouette and you take proper care of it, you can have that suit for a lifetime. It's going to take a lot of cleaning and a lot of wear and tear, but you could put that suit on thirty years from now and you'll still look great—provided you have not also put on thirty pounds. Lay off the Ring Dings, would you?

Suits Are Like Meat:
There Are a Lot of Different Cuts

The American cut. This is also known as the traditional American sack suit. Giggle. I love a sack suit because it's clean and simple; and much like a postcoital smile, it looks great on almost everyone. It's a traditional cut, with a notched lapel and two or three buttons. The jacket has a center vent, and the overall silhouette is lean, with a narrow leg.

The American suit is the Ivy League suit—perfected by makers like Brooks Brothers, J. Press, and Ralph Lauren. It's the suit the Kennedys went to college in. It's also the suit the Kennedys went to traffic court in! Because of its collegiate heritage, a sack suit is considered a casual cut. It looks best with a lot of student debt. Keep it traditional by pairing it with an oxford shirt and a rep tie. It's also great with a T-shirt and sneakers, but that's not for amateurs.

The British cut is similar to the sack suit, with two or three buttons and notched lapels. But whereas a sack suit traditionally comes with a flat-front pant and a center vent, a British suit usually comes with a pleated pant and side vents. Yes, I said pleated pants. Don't be afraid. With this kind of suit, they're allowed.

The Italian and/or double-breasted suit. Traditionally, most Italian suits were double-breasted, hence the name. Just to confuse you, though, Italian suits aren't *always* double-breasted anymore. These days, designers mix and match influences, so you could get an Italian-designed suit in a British silhouette. You could get an American-made suit with an Italian silhouette. The world of fashion is becoming like a Benetton ad. Everybody's mixing it up. Our diversity is making us stronger. And yet, more confused. I feel like the whole world is spinning out of control. What next—are they going to bring back the gaucho?

Anyway, the Italian suit generally has a pleated pant and a wider lapel than the others. The jacket has military origins, and a certain Merrill Stubing elegance about it. In all honesty, this is my least favorite suit. It's just a lot of suit, with a lot of excess material, which is not good for sitting down. If the reason you're wearing a suit is for business meetings at which you'll be seated, it's just not flattering.

This is the suit David Letterman always wears, and the one that always tends to hang open, making the wearer look like he has batwings. Or like he's wearing a cape.

Oh yeah. This is one of the few "you really should be's" you'll ever hear from me, but you really should be tall and slim to wear an Italian suit. One false move and you could look like an extra from *The Sopranos*. A dead extra.

British cut

American sack

Double-breasted

My favorite suit is a charcoal gray pinstriped Etro two-button. What I love about it is that it's very sub-versive. It looks very calm and cool and safe, but that's just a decoy. Still waters run deep, my friends. Because on this suit, the faint pinstripe that would normally be a chalky white is a luscious powdery lavender. And the inside has a zany paisley lining. Call the police—there's a madman in town!

It makes me feel warm all over when I wear it with a striped purple shirt and a black knit tie. Because it gives me that Wall Street kind of feeling of the power suit, but as people get closer, they realize I must work at Rainbow Investments, Ltd.

So if you're in the market to buy that one wedding-and-funeral suit, your best bet is to invest in a classic style and not some flashy fashion suit that will look dated in a year. It shouldn't be a trendy silhouette. It shouldn't have eight buttons or contrast stitching, lapel pins, or rhinestones in the shape of Medusa.

What it should be is a three-button classic British or American silhouette suit (see sidebar) that is going to last you as long as it possibly can—and that you are going to look really, really great in for as long as you possibly can.

Perhaps more so than any other garment you own, suits are about quality over quan-tity. A suit should be one of the most expensive things you buy, and it will most likely have to last you the longest. If you have the sort of job where you need to wear a suit every day, you probably need to look like you know what you're doing. Invest in three or four high-quality suits. If you have the kind of lifestyle where you only need a suit for weddings and funerals, why not invest in one suit of the very best quality you can afford? And you do have to think of it like an investment: If you're willing to spend just a little bit more at the outset, you'll have it forever and won't have to replace or update it four or five times over the years to come. Ultimately, you'll save money. Good grief, I sound positively thrifty.

And let's just get it out of the way, shall we? Here in the U.S., a really good quality, ready-made suit off the rack is going to cost you about $750; a custom handmade suit from a reputable tailor will run upward of $1500. So start clipping those grocery coupons, will you?

I know, I know, you're thinking that you can get a perfectly good suit for $299 at a place like Today's Man. Well, I always say that Today's Man is yesterday's mistake.

You really shouldn't scrimp on a suit. Don't buy a suit that's normally $299 or $399 on the rack at a discount suit warehouse. In fact, avoid buying suits at any place that has the word "warehouse" in its name. Warehouses are best left for things purchased in bulk, like plumbing supplies, lumber, and porn. Not clothing.

If you really don't have a lot of money to spend, department stores have sales twice a year on suits. With some savvy shopping and forward thinking, you could pick up a quality suit at an affordable price, like a fall suit in spring for half off.

What should you be looking for in a suit? Let's talk about fabric first. This is simple. Suits are made of 100 percent wool. It's always the right answer, because you know what you're going to get. There are blends out there, but you just don't know what the materials are. They seem to come up with a new fiber every day. It's like they have people up in their labs twenty-four hours a day inventing the next rayon or gay-lon.

Lightweight wool suits are ideal, because you can wear them in every season. If you only have one suit, that's what you should get. Wool keeps you cool in the summer and warmer in the winter. Because it's a natural fiber, it breathes and keeps you dry. It's easy to care for and it wears well. And the most important thing: It's durable, which is why a good suit can last just about forever.

If you wear a lot of suits, it might be worth investing in a few suits just for summer, in lightweight fabrics like seersucker, poplin, or linen. Seersucker and poplin are made of moisture-wicking cotton, and linen is a kissing cousin of cotton, made from flax. Its texture allows you to feel the breeze through the gauzy weave. (I think that's a Jimmy Buffett song!) It's like the air-conditioned suit, quite frankly. But again, if you're only going to buy one suit, you'll be fine with a lightweight wool year round. In today's climate-controlled world, do we really need to worry about being too hot?

Color

Suits obviously come in many colors and patterns. But if you're that one-suit kind of guy, your best bet is to get a traditional American-cut suit in a solid navy or charcoal gray, or perhaps a classic chalk stripe. Navy and gray are the most versatile, and will allow you to wear endless shirt-and-tie combinations. You can actually renew

TIP

Keep a lint roller handy by your door, right next to wherever you keep your car keys. Just before you go out, especially if you're wearing a dark suit and/or you have an animal friend in your home, you might want to give your suit a little lint roll and spiff yourself up.

your suit every year by just buying a few new shirts and ties. (Yes, this requires the occasional shopping outing. Good times!)

A general note about all suits: Keep the color palette simple and traditional. A mustard-colored suit à la MC Hammer is so very rarely the right look. When I see someone in a mustard-colored suit, I'm tempted to say, "Pardon me, do you have any, um, taste?" Save the mustard colors and eggplants and aubergines for sassy sport coats to be worn during the summer months in the hot resort spots of Nantucket, Catalina, or Omaha.

I'd also steer away from the black suit unless you have many suits to choose from. Black can be very, very severe, and/or a little flashy and a little showy. Paired with a white shirt and a black tie, you'll undoubtedly look like the limo driver at the wedding or the only Amish mourner at the funeral. The only exception is when you're the groom at a semiformal wedding. Then a black suit is cool.

Though I've tried to keep this book from being too technical for you, you do need to know a little bit about how a suit jacket is constructed and the details to look for. I promise this won't hurt and will be over before you know it. Just hold on and have a Ritalin smoothie, okay?

DETAIL #1 The Shoulder

The most important detail on any suit is the shoulder. Why? Because constructing a suit is an art. You're taking a two-dimensional fabric and turning it into a three-dimensional object. It's like a sculpture made of sewing.

The way that the shoulder meets the armhole (that sounds really kinky) is going to affect how the rest of the jacket fits. In a well-tailored shoulder, the sleeve will fit smoothly into the armhole at every point, with little or no puckering.

bad shoulder

good shoulder

Sometimes when you see a bad suit, it almost looks like it's pleated around the arm-hole, or it looks like a woman's suit sleeve with a bit of a puff to it. That's exactly what you don't want. You want it to be almost seamless, so that the jacket doesn't pull at all.

Unfortunately, it's really difficult to finesse that, especially if the suit is not sewn by hand—and almost every suit that you buy off the rack in a department store or discount store is going to be machine made. But there are some machine-made suits out there—by designers like Calvin Klein, Brooks Brothers, Ralph Lauren, and even some more modest brands—that really look like they're hand-sewn. You just have to look for them.

DETAIL #2 Buttons and Buttonholes

The buttons on your suit jacket should be made of natural materials like horn. Plastic buttons are always a no, because during various dry cleanings and whatnot, plastic will deteriorate and crack and become brittle. How can you tell if your buttons are plastic or horn? Plastic buttons will be shiny and uniform in color. But horn buttons are marbled in appearance, like a good cut of beef.

The buttonholes on a well-made suit will be clean and neat and tight. You should test them out by fastening and unfastening the button a few times. The buttons should just barely fit in the buttonhole and should stay fairly snug; they shouldn't have too much room. The holes themselves shouldn't have any frays or any loose threads. Loose threads only indicate that the buttonhole will have a tendency to unravel. You'll be in a real pinch if you have a problem with your hole.

On a really, really high-end suit jacket, you'll find working buttons and buttonholes on the sleeves, so that you can actually open and close them at the cuffs. These are sometimes called doctors' cuffs. Originally, when doctors were working on patients, they would wear a jacket and they would have to roll up their sleeves, so as not to get who knows what on their suit. (Amaze your buddies on trivia night at Joe's Bar!) There is no longer a practical use for doctors' cuffs and it's a very expensive detail that most suits just don't have anymore. I just wanted to share.

DETAIL #3 The Lining and Interlining

A good suit should have a full lining, meaning the entire interior, including the sleeves, will be lined. The best linings are silk, but a nice rayon will work as well. A suit lining helps with moisture and creates a barrier between the actual suit and your body. It also allows you to improve the fit of the suit, as slippery silk makes everything drape better. And it makes the suit jacket easier to put on and take off. If your suit is not fully lined, when you slip your arms in the armholes, there will be friction with your shirtsleeve. That can make the jacket hard to get into, not to mention cause extra wrinkling. And we all know how unfortunate that can be.

Examine the lining to make sure it's all sewn beautifully and tacked down. If the lining is loose or shabby or cheap, that's an indicator of a lesser-quality jacket.

A good suit jacket should also have an interlining to give it structure. The interlining is like a little woven grid, kind of like a teeny-weeny miniaturized latch-hook rug, that is sewn into the shoulders and the chest of a jacket. It's the armature or "bones" of the suit that keep it properly proportioned and help give it a permanent three-dimensional shape and structure. The interlining allows places that need to drape to drape and makes sure that the places that shouldn't drape don't. It's the "looks like a pump, feels like a sneaker" mentality at its finest.

Think of a sandwich: If the outer fabric the suit jacket is made of is the top piece of bread, and the inner lining is the bottom piece of bread, the interlining is the ham and cheese sewn in between—except it's hidden away where you won't be able to see it. But you can feel for it and you'll know it's there. Hopefully.

A cheap suit may not have an interlining at all, or if it does have one, it might be bad quality, made of plastic or other synthetic materials that aren't going to breathe and last.

Keep in mind that there is something known as an unconstructed suit, which won't have an interlining or shoulder pads, and might not even have a regular lining. This is a "look," but I highly recommend you step away. Unconstructed suits have a very easy breezy "Yanni at the Acropolis" flair. The unconstructed sport coat, on the other hand, can be a great, easy, and relaxed look. (See the next section, "Sport Coats.")

DETAIL #4 Patterns

If the suit you're considering has a pattern like a tattersall or glen plaid, a houndstooth, a herringbone, or a Pound Puppies print—no, scratch that last one—you should check to make sure all the patterns match up where the seams meet. It's just like the repeat of wallpaper—the pattern should be seamless. If the pattern doesn't match up, that's the sign of a suit that's less than top shelf.

DETAIL #5 The Pockets

Suit jacket pockets should be lined and functional. They should also actually be there and not just an optical illusion. Sometimes a cheap suit will just have the flap on the outside, but no actual pocket. And that's quite a surprise when you go to slip in your Tic Tacs!

On a good quality suit, you'll need to cut the jacket pockets open, preferably with a nail scissor or something similar. Do not rip them open or use a chainsaw. Your tailor can do this for you while you're having your suit tailored.

Now that we've got your suit jacket under control, next come the pants. To cuff or not to cuff, that is the question. Cuffs really don't serve a purpose anymore. Once upon a time, when you were traipsing around on muddy streets in the London or New York of olden days, you would just roll your pants up a little bit to protect them. When more people began wearing suits as the business uniform, this impromptu cuff was incorporated as a standard feature of the suit. In today's modern world of clean sidewalks and efficient municipal waste systems, those cuffs are obsolete, unless you live in Walnut Grove. In which case I suggest you head over to Doc Baker's and get some of that new drug everyone's talking about. I think they call it "aspirin"??

Cuffs are strictly a matter of personal taste. For a traditional American- or English-cut suit, I like them. They look finished. They belong there. They're a matter of tradition, particularly a one-and-a-quarter- or one-and-a-half-inch cuff. Suit pants can be a longer than dress pants, with more of a break. This means that more fabric can be pooling when you're standing upright. The goal is to avoid showing a lot of ankle or calf when you're seated in a suit. The less leg showing, the more elegant, and a suit is obviously more elegant than dress pants.

If the pants have pleats—and yes, for some very traditional suits I can still endorse a pleat—they should definitely have cuffs as well. But for cleaner, more modern suits, especially Italian suits, I like a flat-front pant. And if pants have a flat-front, they shouldn't have cuffs. It just looks more clean and sophisticated. Cuffed flat-front pants look a little too Mickey Rooney—or like you should be out selling newspapers with Oliver Twist.

BLAZERS OR SPORT COATS

If you're not a suit wearer, but you have the occasion to get dressed up now and again for a dinner date or a party, you should have a couple of good blazers in your wardrobe.

Blazers are super, super versatile. You can wear a blazer with anything. Wear it with jeans. Dress it up with tweed pants. Wear it with a dress shirt. Wear it with culottes. Wear it with a micromini. Wear it with lederhosen! Okay, maybe not those last few.

For your first blazer, I recommend a navy blue, lightweight wool for all seasons—even summer. Nothing looks cooler or more classically chic than a blue blazer, a pink oxford and a pair of khakis. You can dress it up with a fun pocket square if you don't want to wear a tie.

Just like a good suit, a classic blue blazer is an investment. You're going to have it forever. You can buy a proper blue blazer when you're twenty and have it through your Viagra years. Ah, Viagra. Ain't life grand?

tweed and denim

blue blazer and jeans

corduroy and military

A blue blazer can have plain horn buttons or traditional brass ones, either plain or with a monogram. Plain horn buttons are more versatile, but I love the tradition and the heritage of the brass. If you're buying good quality, the buttons should be subtle, not super shiny and garish.

Try to think outside the box with your blue blazer. It's very European to wear a sport coat with all sorts of things, for all seasons, all times of day, and all occasions. Think about all the many ways you can dress it up: with a sweater, with a tie, with a dress shirt. Or dress it down with jeans or cargo pants. You can do so many things with it. It slices, it dices, it cubes, it juliennes your favorite vegetables—just like the Ginsu!

For fall and winter, you should have a tweed blazer. This one will be rugged but warm and is always stylish. And don't think that you can only pair a tweed blazer with an oxford shirt and a pipe. Try wearing it in an updated way, with a skinny cashmere sweater underneath or a rock-and-roll T-shirt. Wear it with jeans—it looks great.

If you want to be nutty, you can invest in a corduroy blazer as well. I have a certain fetish for elbow patches that stems from having seen Ryan O'Neal in *Love Story* a few too many times. But that's another book . . . in which I play the role of Ali MacGraw. Sigh.

ONE CARDINAL RULE: You don't want to wear pants and a sport coat that try to make it look like you're wearing a suit. You're not fooling anyone. Don't match your slacks to your blazer; you'll look like you work at Subway. Avoid quirky colors. It's not the place to get quirky. (Century 21 agents exempted.) Oh, and do me a favor and make sure your blazers fit, okay? They shouldn't be like sacks (the bags, not the store).

TIES AND POCKET SQUARES

There is nothing that can kill a great outfit, even if it's a stunning handmade suit, like a bad tie. A lot of guys see ties as an afterthought, but ties are so important. If you are going to wear one, especially in this day and age when nobody's wearing them—it better be sensational.

You really need to take care of your ties and make sure that they're good-looking and smart, but ties can also be fun. They can give a hint of your personality, or make a gentle nod to something that you enjoy, like sailboats or vintage cars. Just don't take

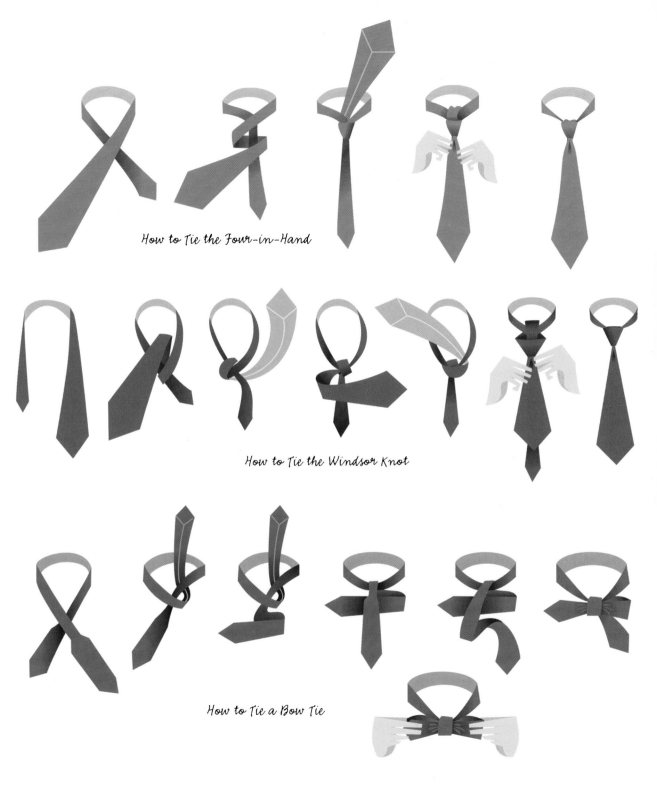

How to Tie the Four-in-Hand

How to Tie the Windsor Knot

How to Tie a Bow Tie

In 1991, right after college graduation, I got my first job and moved to New York. And my very first winter in the big city, I sold neckwear at Saks Fifth Avenue over the holidays.

Neckwear is the total bottom rung for men's clothing. It's the one place where all people who don't know what they want come to buy a gift. They say, "I just don't know. I'll get him a tie!" It's so lame. But I'm sure I touched many lives. I can just see them even now, in some tony apartment on the Upper East Side, opening that gift box to find hot pink whales on a green cotton background. And some guy in a tweed blazer would say, "Thanks for the tie, Joan. Where'd you find this one?" And she would answer, "This cute little blond guy picked it out for me at Saks!" I really got a sense of satisfaction from helping people find themselves through clothes. That has always been my thing, and I really believe that much of it started right there, in the neckwear department of Saks. Now I'm a little verklempt, are you? It was a happy, magical time.

that too far. You don't want to get a tie that has toy trucks all over it, or Christmas trees that light up.

People ask how to find a good tie, but it's kind of like when you see a puppy at the animal shelter: When it's the right one, you'll know it. One very simple thing to keep in mind is that ties should always be made of silk. There's one slight exception: Very, very English ties for fall are sometimes made of wool challis. They're very sophisticated, but they're not easy to find and you might not even come across them. I also love knit ties, very Alex P. Keaton, but very chic when done tone-on-tone with a sophisticated suit. But they're not for everybody.

A good practice when tie shopping is to give the tie a good feel. A good tie will have an inner construction that is actually tangible. If you took it apart, there would be something like a piece of mesh or screen that gives it some body and structure. A bad tie is wimpy and soft. If you make a quick knot, you'll see it won't hold a dimple, which should warn you that your dimple is going to flatten out when you wear it. Major chubby killer!

With so many tie variations out there, it would be impossible to make any lists of ties you must own or tell you how to pick patterns. Just remember that ties are, once again, a great place to keep it simple. The classic rep tie, which often has a regi-mental stripe, can be very bright and preppy or quite subdued and elegant. You can never go wrong with a rep tie. Practically as effective as an Ivy League education for a mere fraction of the cost!

And finally, a lot of guys don't realize that certain ties relate to certain seasons. Muted rusts, gold, rich reds, and wool ties lend themselves much more to fall and winter. A lime-green-and-navy rep tie paired with a pink oxford would be much more appropriate for spring and summer.

What Color Is Your Pocket Square?

Forget your parachute. The burning question these days is "What color is your pocket square?" Pocket squares really just add that extra little tszuj to an outfit, especially if you're wearing a blazer and you're not wearing a tie. You can look nekkid without it. **REMEMBER:** You always want to look distinguished and ahead of the pack. As far as I'm concerned, you might as well not even wear pants if you're not wearing a pocket square.

Pocket squares should be made of silk—or cotton for summer—but silk is always best. Cotton may look a little too dicey. And for heaven's sake, do not blow your nose in them. It's not a hankie or a snot rag, people. Please, do yourself a favor and grab a Puffs instead.

An easy way to pick a pocket square is to remember it should pull out one color of an item you're wearing—a stripe or pattern. If you're wearing a blue blazer and a pale blue-and-white striped shirt, for instance, maybe your pocket square would be pale blue.

How to Fold a Pocket Square

When it comes to folding the pocket square, I like them to be natural looking. I don't like when it's all neatly folded. It's not origami. Those three pointy triangles you sometimes see poking out of a local news anchor's jacket? Way too fussy, in my opinion. Notice that he's also wearing a pinky ring and a gold rope chain bracelet. Capice?

You just want to lay your pocket square flat on a table. Pinch right in the middle between your thumb and forefinger and let it hang naturally—it will sort of look like a little ghost. Make a circle with the thumb and forefinger of your other hand, and draw the "ghost" through. Flip it over, fold it in half, and stick it in the pocket. You should have a little bit of the rounded front part and a little bit of the tail sticking out. It's an art form, so practice makes perfect.

THE FINISHED SUIT LOOK: PULLING IT ALL TOGETHER

Oooh, that sounds naughty, doesn't it? That's bringing back Boy Scout jamboree memories, people. In tents. I mean intense.

Anyway, I know you're confused. You've got a great classic suit. You have great shirts. You have some good ties and pocket squares. Now what? Three little words, peanut! Color, pattern, and scale. You can harmonize everything through just those three things. It's just like making a martini. All it takes is finesse, practice, and good credit.

Your Friend, the Tailor

Your neighborhood tailor should become one of your best friends. The tailor is an important professional, just like your doctor, but the licensing requirements are not quite as stringent. Anyone can hang up a shingle and call him- or herself a tailor. You have to find the good ones by word of mouth. So if you move to a new area, you need to ask friends, get recommendations, or you need to go and test tailors out by having a shirt altered or pants cuffed. Don't take your new expensive suit to a brand-new tailor. If you're buying a suit, and the store doesn't do its own tailoring, ask the salesperson who they recommend. Generally this is a great way to find a reliable tailor.

Let's start, for example, with a charcoal gray suit. Add one accent color in the dress shirt like pink, light blue, or lavender. (White is so boring!) The shirt could also have a pattern, like a small gridlike windowpane, a faint herringbone, or a tone-on-tone design; or it could be a stripe.

The tie adds pattern and dimension. When mixing patterns, it's all about complementary scale. The scale of the tie pattern should be bolder than the scale of the shirt pattern and should pick up color references from both the suit (charcoal gray) and the shirt (lavender, pink, or blue). It's as easy as $e = mc^2$. You do the math! Now just add a white pocket square for a dash of formality, or choose one that coordinates with—but doesn't match—the necktie. It's a little too "I work at Avis" when it all matches.

Always the Wrong Answer . . .

Pastel suits. They've gone the way of Miami Vice and Don Johnson's career.

Shiny suits. You never want to look like a walking baked potato.

Leisure suits. It's an oxymoron, people.

Double-breasted blue blazers with anchors on the buttons. You are not the captain of the Good Ship Lollipop. Your blue blazer should be single breasted.

Bow ties with suits. Just a little too Orville Redenbacher.

Cravats and ascots. Unless you're trying out for the part of Thurston Howell III or are a member of a royal imperial court.

Novelty ties

Bolo ties

It's a Wrap
JACKETS, SCARVES, GLOVES, AND HATS

YOUR OUTERWEAR (OR A GIGANTIC ZIT: SEE CHAPTER NINE) IS THE FIRST THING PEOPLE SEE WHEN THEY MEET YOU, SO PAY attention. You could be wearing a barrel with suspenders underneath—hell, you could be *naked* underneath—but if you have a nice-looking jacket on, people are only going to say, "Heeeeey! Looking good!" On the flip side, an inappropriate jacket— like a casual barn coat over a beautiful custom-made suit—can shut you down like a bad Ferris wheel. You could be wearing the most gorgeous suit in the world, but if you throw on a bad coat, game over. It's like putting t-tops and fuzzy dice on a Rolls.

To make it even easier for you, I, your personal fashion life coach, will now tell you the seven coats I think you need to own. It's that simple.

1. A denim jacket. **Why? Because it's an American icon. A legend. It's rugged, cool, and stylish. It's James Dean. It adds a nice twist to your wardrobe, and you can wear it six months out of the year. If you're a little dressed up and you throw the denim jacket on, instant cool. Plus—bonus, kids!—it's affordable because it's cotton: the fabric of our lives.**

The denim jacket is an amazing layering piece. It looks fantastic over a sweater or under a blazer. You've probably never done anything as crazy as wear a denim jacket under a

blazer, but it works. Just trust me. Sometimes you need to try the unconventional and just see what it looks like. If you hate it, you can put your Cliff Huxtable collectible Coogi sweater back on, but you might be pleasantly surprised.

Note to self (you, not me): You don't want to pair a denim jacket with matching denim pants, or you'll look like a denim-peddling ice-cream man. But with just about everything else it looks fantastic.

Just like we talked about with jeans, you want to avoid the fashion denim jacket and steer toward something like a classic Levi's jacket. Anything that's shiny, coated, or anything that's been Be-Dazzled is to be avoided. And I know. I was addicted to Be-Dazzling for seven years. It's the great enabler—worse than crack cocaine. I don't even have any Be-Dazzled creations left to share. It's like dumping all the booze down the drain when you get sober: You have to get rid of it all.

Ah, but I digress. Back to your jean jacket. You should buy them basically true to fit, maybe a smidge larger than you'd normally wear because you might want to layer with a sweater. The armholes should be high, and the jacket should button snugly in the front. People tend to buy denim jackets oversized, but that's to be avoided, unless you want to look like an extra from *Saved By the Bell* or *Sixteen Candles*.

2. A peacoat. Every man should have a peacoat in his closet. It's a classic, born of a great military tradition that's stood the test of time. And in my book, anything that manages to get from the military to the gay man's wardrobe has got to be good. Don't ask, I'll tell.

The classic peacoat comes in dark-as-midnight navy blue wool and is military inspired. You can buy the real thing from an army/navy surplus store. Or you can buy a fashion version from a designer. The fashion version might be a little cuddlier and more comfortable, and might be leaner in cut. But it's your choice—either's fine.

Peacoats are warm and sophisticated, and look great with anything from jeans to a suit. They can be very dressed up or very casual. Guys look hot in them. Think of Marlon Brando in *On the Waterfront*. Hello! I came *this* close to joining the navy because of that look. I found myself at the recruiting office, only to learn that fashion options are somewhat limited in the military. "What is all this white after Labor Day?" I politely inquired. "It's the uniform," the recruiter answered. "As in, dressed like everybody else?" I asked in horror. "No, thank you!" So I marched right out of there and over to Saks Fifth Avenue, where, lucky for you and our national security, I began a career in neckwear instead.

You might occasionally see peacoats out there in different fabrics and colors beyond basic navy wool. That's the thing about fashion; it's always reinventing itself. It's the designer's job to innovate—to dream up new interpretations.

You'll see peacoats in cashmere or leather or nylon. Those are all great options if you're going to invest in more than one. If you're just getting one, make it classic. Because after wearing that orange-nylon-and-corduroy peacoat you thought was such a fun twist on a fashion basic just a couple of times, you might get sick of it and long for a simple navy wool one.

3. A windbreaker. You need to have the right outerwear for the right season, and for spring and fall, a windbreaker is a nice, light jacket that's going to do the job for you. One thing I hate to see is someone suffering from seasonal dyslexia—you know, wearing a fur coat and earmuffs when it's fifty-five degrees out. Now, I love sheared beaver as much as the next guy, but there is a time and a place for everything. (For more on that, see chapter nine.) A jacket is meant to keep you warm and dry and comfortable, and those needs will change from season to season. Your jacket shouldn't make you sweat like Jim and Tammy Faye Bakker at tax time.

I know I sound like a broken record, but when it comes to the windbreaker, it's really important to keep it simple. It should be light and lean and mean, and should do its job of chill chasing without detracting from the rest of your look. A good windbreaker should be made of a lightweight luxury nylon—yes, there is such a thing as luxury nylon, just ask your friendly sales associate—or coated cotton twill. I like a short plain-front zip-up that's not too fussy, maybe with two slash pockets. (Those are pockets without flaps, people.)

While it's very tempting, especially in spring, to buy an orange or bright blue windbreaker, take a step back, take a deep breath, and realize that neutral-colored windbreakers are always going to serve you best. Remember that they have to work in both spring and fall. Navy, black, and khaki are all good choices. Avoid white because you can only use it for spring, unless you're planning on enrolling in a shuffleboard league in Boca.

4. A topcoat. This is the fancy overcoat you'll wear over a suit. Think about Cary Grant and those classic suits he would wear. He *always* had a topcoat and he *always* looked cool. A topcoat is made to fit like a suit, because it *is* a suit. It's the third piece to a suit. (Or the fourth if you're Uncle Wiggly.)

You want to look for an overcoat made of natural fibers: wool, camel hair or—cha-ching!—cashmere if you dare, in a simple, conservative charcoal gray, navy, or camel. Beyond that, consider the exact same things you would look for in choosing a suit. (See chapter five.) A topcoat is just like a long suit coat made of thicker wool material. Inspect the buttonholes, the lining, the shoulder construction, the stitching. Just like on a suit jacket, the buttons on a good overcoat should be a natural material like horn, not plastic.

The sleeves of a topcoat need to be longer than your suit and your shirt, because they're meant to protect them. Ideally, your coat should extend about a half inch beyond your suit sleeves. As for the length, three-quarter length topcoats, which come to the knee, are acceptable only if you're on the shorter side, because a full-length coat will drown you. Men who are average height or taller should invest in a full-length topcoat, which hits from just below the knee to halfway down the calf. It shouldn't be so long that it restricts you in walking or makes you look like a friar going to vespers. Speaking of friars, you might want to avoid brown topcoats, so that nobody asks you for directions to the local monastery or for a spot of Frangelico.

Take Off the Labels, People!

If you are wearing an overcoat or a suit jacket that comes with an outer label stitched onto the forearm or wrist area, please put down this book and go clip it off. And for God's sake use a nail clipper and not scissors, so you don't cut a hole in your fabulous new coat.

5. **Tell me about leather, Daddy.** (The leather jacket.) A leather jacket is an important addition to your closet because it adds just a little bit of ruggedness and flair to your look. It takes things from being just a little wimpy and adds a real toughness to them, which I love. And just like Asian women, good-quality leather will age beautifully.

Keep in mind, though, that if you live somewhere with really brutal winters, a leather jacket is probably not going to be your best bet for a primary winter coat. Because leather is skin, it conducts temperature rather than truly insulates. It will never be as warm as wool or cashmere, which can actually trap air in between the weave of the fibers.

When it comes to a leather jacket, you want to look for a classic motorcycle jacket—think James Dean, not Fonzie—a leather peacoat, or a three-quarter-length car coat. Just avoid the bomber jacket at all costs. *Top Gun* had its moment, and it's over. So let's let it rest peacefully.

Look for good quality leather. It's like the quality of booze, which some of the more fashion-phobic among you can probably relate to. You can buy really cheap house brands, or you can invest in top shelf. A good leather jacket really *is* an investment, because if it's high quality and a classic silhouette, and you'll have it for the rest of your life. Just like that nasty little rash you picked up in Cancun.

Here's my quick lesson in leather. (Oooh! I always wanted to say that.) Before you do anything else, first check the tag and see that the jacket really is leather. Leather is a very generic term for anything made from the hide of an animal; there are tons of variables. It could be goat leather, cowhide, pigskin, or even horsehide. (Holy Mr. Ed! Let's hope not.) So first and foremost, make sure it's natural. Good leather should be soft and supple, which means that when you bend it, it should flex and not crack.

Just like other garments, the lining of a leather jacket will also tell a story. The quality of the lining, as in how good a job they did stitching it in, will tell you a lot about the overall quality, because the lining is one place where inferior manufacturers feel like they can cut corners.

As for distressed leather, I think it's super if the jacket is naturally distressed from wear or you're buying a vintage piece, but generally any kind of engineered distressing or leather treatment is going to be the wrong answer. Fashion victim, party of one? Your table's ready.

6. Nylon sports jacket or parka. You should definitely have a warm three-quarter-length sports-inspired jacket in a luxury nylon—something that resists the elements and can be dressed up or dressed down. This is the jacket you'll wear when you're casually dressed and the weather's truly inclement, and you might not want to wear suede or wool or leather.

You want to keep the color story simple and opt for classics like black, steel gray, or brown. Avoid bright colors and lime green, because that will make you look like Suzy Chaffee. I also hate to see guys running around town in authentic ski jackets with the lift tickets still hanging on them. Let's save those for the hill, people. Invest in a ski jacket or some kind of nylon outerwear that will look great on the slopes and is also great for the city. The North Face puffer jacket is a perfect example of something that looks at home in either

Wearing fabrics that invite touch, like cashmere, suede, and leather, is better than buying girls a drink. Touchable fabrics make people want to come up and cuddle you, provided you don't have a great big cold sore on your lip. For that I highly recommend a trip to your local drugstore to pick up some Valtrex.

setting. It's a classic that's innocuous enough to mix with sportswear, but you can also ski with it and it's totally functional. I also love RLX jackets (by Ralph Lauren) and Victorinox jackets, both of which look equally great with suits (business *and* ski).

7. **Trenchcoats.** Just because it's raining outside doesn't mean that you have to ruin a perfectly good outfit with a horrible trenchcoat. There's no need to look like a flasher or McGruff the Crime Dog. Invest in one good quality raincoat that's chic and sophisticated, not one in that horrible putty color that every insurance adjuster from here to Des Moines has on. And for God's sake don't let me catch you with the belts flapping in the breeze. It's just a sad, sad commuter look that is always the wrong answer.

When it comes to raincoats, always opt for a darker color. A dark golden khaki is so much richer than that overused putty. And get one with a lining that snaps in and out. That way you can wear it on colder winter days or in spring and fall.

Oh, and while we're at it, let me just remind you that shiny yellow slickers are so not cool. You'll look like the Morton's salt girl or the Gorton's fisherman. I would also avoid umbrellas that look like frogs, or galoshes shaped like ladybugs. Unless your daily commute involves a yellow school bus. Then, by all means, indulge.

SCARVES AND GLOVES AND HATS, OH MY!

Scarves

If you can dream it, you can crochet it. And unfortunately, that's exactly what your great-aunt Tillie from Milwaukee did on her Knitaway—available from Ronco, free with the Be-Dazzler, circa 1979—when she gave you that multicolored scarf now hanging in your closet. (I have a storage unit full of Knitaways because I bought so many Be-Dazzlers, by the way. Hello? eBay?)

Great-aunt Tillie seems to be the source for most men's scarves. Scarves just seem to come into our lives. You don't realize how you get them, you just get them. They're like moles.

But just like everything else, you need to *buy* scarves. You need to have a classic, basic scarf. I recommend a black or gray cashmere scarf—it's a great introduction to cashmere at about $75. They're warm, chic, and sophisticated, and they look great with everything. You can wear them with a suit, with a casual sweater, or even jeans and a T-shirt. Those crazy multicolored scarves that you get from great-aunt Tillie? Those don't look good with *anything*.

The scarf is a big holiday gift, but inevitably you get the one you don't want. Time to go shopping! After the holidays there are vast quantities of scarves on sale, although selection might be slightly limited. But in most climates, that's just when you're going to need one, and you might hit a great deal.

If you can't do cashmere, look for merino wool or superfine lambswool. But whatever you do, keep the fibers real, just like everything else. Avoid scarves made of things like "cashmayre" or "cashmink" or "cashmina." It's a plot to trick you. But alas, dear reader, you've got me on your side, and you shan't be duped.

Watch out for novelty scarves, too. If it lights up, plays music, is decorated with a keyboard, or is adorned with any Disney characters whatsoever, just keep looking.

Gloves

Let's just come right out and say it: Mittens are for preschoolers. Yes, they keep you the warmest, but who really needs to be *that* warm? They also make you unable to do anything. Wearing mittens is a great excuse for never doing a thing. Witness the following.

"Could you get that for me?"

"Nope! Got mittens on!"

"Could you answer the phone?"

"No, sorry, mittens."

"Could you drive tonight?"

"I'd love to, but I'm wearing mittens."

As with all things, your best bet is to keep your gloves simple. If you find one classic pair you can wear with anything, you'll be set. If you work at a job where you wear work gloves to protect your hands, that's great, but those are not the gloves I'm talking about. For going out on a date or going out with friends on a weekend, what you want is a simple, real leather glove—ideally with a thin lining of wool or cashmere to add extra insulation without being bulky and lumberjack-y.

Gloves should be either brown or black. Think about your outerwear. If your coats are mostly black, get black gloves. If they're mostly brown, do brown. Now, was that so difficult?

For the record, matching your gloves and your coat does not mean you need to match your hat, scarf, and shoes, unless you're also carrying a handbag or you want to look like Lana Turner. In that case, it's fine, and don't forget to wear a mink stole. Otherwise, don't be so worried. It doesn't have to match. Coordinated, yes. Matching, no.

And we certainly hope you aren't using those clips that attach your gloves to your coat. If you need those, you're worse off than you thought.

Hats

Let's face it. The reason most men wear hats is not to look suave, and not to look sophisticated, but because they're having a BHD, the inevitable bad-hair day. But look on the bright side. It's better than the no-hair day. Still, hats shouldn't be worn just as a cover-up. Hats add so much style and flair, and they keep your noggin warm. I will warn you to proceed with caution: Hats can make you look absolutely fabulous or like a complete jackass. You can never go wrong with the basics, but I don't want you getting mixed up with designer fashion hats. The next thing you know you'll be subscribing to *Playgirl*.

Here's my list of some good hats…and some to avoid.

GOOD HATS

1. **Ballcaps.** A ballcap can provide a cute sporty look in the right situation—say, it's the weekend or you're going to the movies. But please—puh-leeze—take it off when indoors. Just be careful that they're not overly logoed or gigantic, with a huge rise. The closer your baseball cap is to a beanie, the better off you probably are. (See foam truckers under "Bad Hats.")

2. **Newsboy caps.** I love the newsboy cap that's become really popular lately. It's quite fetching on most men and can add a lot of panache. It looks great with a woven shirt and a sport coat. Just please don't wear these with a tweed suit or you'll look like Mickey Rooney in *National Velvet*.

3. **Knit caps.** You should definitely have a nice warm knit cap for the winter, specifically a skullcap in black, brown, or gray wool. That means it's not a ski hat with a pom-pom on the end. Those are best for the ski mountain or for *Ice Castles*

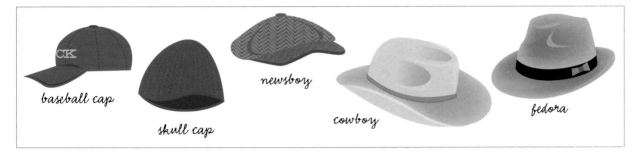

baseball cap

skull cap

newsboy

cowboy

fedora

GOOD HATS

theme night in the privacy of your own home. If you're actually skiing, you're excused, because half the fun of skiing is getting dressed up in the outfit. I also love a hot toddy in the lodge *après* ski. Or a hot David or Billy for that matter.

4. **Fedoras.** I fully endorse them and would love to see them come back, but I don't think women will start wearing gloves again, either. They look especially great with a suit, but just make sure they're not huge. Okay, here's an advanced maneuver: There are seasonal rules for hats, too. Natural straw (aka the Panama) is for spring and summer, and beaver (yes, beaver) is for fall and winter.

5. **Cowboy hats.** The cowboy hat is a personal favorite of mine, hearkening back to my days as a trick rider on the gay rodeo circuit. Ah, but that was a lifetime and many broken nails ago.

It's an American icon, like the cowboy boot. Just be careful it doesn't look like a party favor you'd get at an overproduced Western-themed bar mitzvah. It should be authentic. It should be well worn and weathered, and made of natural straw and not recycled things like tires or soda cans.

tin can

beer can helmut

ski hat with pom-pom

foam trucker cap

BAD HATS

BAD HATS

1. Foam truckers. **Avoid the foam trucker unless you're Ashton Kutcher, and he's so darn cute that I'll let him get away with it. The reason that the rise of a foam trucker is so big is so that they can put a billboard on your head, complete with a logo, phone number, map, e-mail address, and store hours. If there's room to print every store location nationwide, your hat is too damn big. In other words? Trucker hats: best left for truckers.**

2. Kangol and hipster hats. **Those funky, updated berets—favored by Samuel L. Jackson and the late John F. Kennedy Jr.—are really way trendy and probably don't look good on too many people. Definitely not for amateurs, and best left to Alicia Keys.**

3. Novelty fleece ski hats that make you look like you have dreadlocks or make you look like a pterodactyl. **It's a no-brainer, like the people who still wear them. Acceptable in Canada.**

4. Any hats purchased while drunk at Mardi Gras. **I don't care what it looks like. Just get rid of it.**

5. **Do rags and bandanna "drug helmets."** They look good on Nelly, but then again, what doesn't? Chocolate thunder!

6. **Jester hats.** They were invented to make people laugh at you. Brilliant invention. Still works!

7. **Hats that combine the art of crochet with the art of recycling.** You've seen them at county fairs: shards of old Mountain Dew cans lovingly (or drunkenly) strewn together with neon-colored yarn to create a conversational-but-stomach-wrenching bucket hat. Your green, earth-friendly impulses are to be applauded, but not at the expense of polluting the fashion landscape with ugly headwear. I'm channeling that sad Indian again.

BLACK & WHITE CHIC

7

Accessories

LAST THING ON, FIRST THING NOTICED

STYLISH ACCESSORIES ARE SO VERY IMPORTANT. JUST BECAUSE THEY'RE SMALL AND GO ON LAST DOESN'T MEAN THAT THEY should be an afterthought or that you can go without them. Think of accessories as the crowning glory of that wardrobe you've worked so hard to put together: You need to pay attention and not screw them up.

JEWELRY

A RULE: What is worn in Vegas should stay in Vegas.

The average straight man's jewelry should be minimal. Most of the time, men and jewelry just don't mix. Unless you've won a Super Bowl, there is no reason to wear a giant dome ring as an homage to your gridiron glory days. Put it in your hope chest or hock it. Chains, rings, anything like that—especially when done in gold—will always make you look like you're in the Mafia or trying out for *Kiss Me, Guido*.

If you're a young guy, or exceptionally cool, a simple necklace made of a piece of suede cording with a little piece of silver hanging from it—either a small cross or some sort of ethnic token—can look really hot with an open shirt, or with a T-shirt and denim. It's very rock and roll. Very Johnny Depp. Just remember that whatever's hanging from the cord should *never* be bigger than your head or a toaster. Come to think of it, your head shouldn't be bigger than a toaster, either.

As for earrings, I'll be honest: I don't like them. For 99.9 percent of men, I think earrings make you look like an out-of-date rock star or a pirate, and neither is a particularly enviable look. In very rare instances, someone like Johnny Depp or Lenny Kravitz can get away with earrings. But for average Joes, I suggest you take that earring out and leave your Def Leppard fantasy at the door, thank you. My motto? Studs without studs.

The only jewelry I will unconditionally allow, of course, is a wedding band. That's the kind of sacred ground where I could never say what's good and what's bad. It's so special, and obviously, if you have one on, you've received it before I've gotten to you. Hopefully you're wearing a simple, classic, elegant wedding band, but even if you're not, the person who gave it to you loves you and you still have to wear it no matter what I say. I'll deal.

WATCHES

Because most men don't wear jewelry, thank God, a great watch is really important. Unless you're a gender illusionist (or drag queen, as some people so mundanely call them), a nice watch should be the most noticeable piece of jewelry you own. Your watch doesn't have to be a Rolex. But it shouldn't cost $5.99 and be made of plastic or held together with Scotch tape, either. Think somewhere in the middle of those two extremes. You can get a great watch like a Swatch that's relatively inexpensive and looks amazing. Actually, get two watches: one for work and one for the weekend. When they're classic and sophisticated, they will last you a lifetime. I love a classic diving watch, a chronograph in stainless steel, or for a more dressy option that looks great, a tank watch.

Another great trick is to buy a watch with a simple silver or stainless steel case and a removable band. You can have a brown leather band, a crocodile band, and even a fun multicolored grosgrain one for summer. It's a great way to get many different looks out of one watch. Versatile. Like me!

For the record, I don't mind a sports watch, I just recommend you don't overly trick them out. Your watch

When it comes to designer knockoffs, men don't fall into as many traps as women do. But the one place in the marketplace you will find designer imitations for men is in accessories—watches, shoes, belts, and luggage.

If you're buying a Rolex for $50 from a guy on the corner who also sells incense and windup barking dog toys, I have news for you: It's not real. I would much rather see you buy a cool, well-engineered, great-looking Swatch for fifty bucks than have you wear a fake Rolex. It isn't who you are, it's pretentious, and—oh yeah—it's illegal! If you are a Rolex kind of guy, that's great, but buy the genuine article. Buying a fake Rolex is like having sex on the Internet. It's not real.

The real thing costs more because it *is* the real thing—you're paying for construction, classic design, and overall quality. When you buy a fake, you're not getting any of that. I'm not going to get all PC (politically Carson) on you, but the bottom line is you get what you pay for. Even I've bought fakes, I confess, but they're never worth it.

shouldn't be able to land the space shuttle or locate a stolen car. It's a watch, not a LoJack.

Guys should also think about the scale of their watch in ratio to the size of their wrists. You don't want a big hunking piece of metal if you have a skinny little chicken-bone wrist. You know what they say: big wrists . . . big watch. Once again, invoke the head rule: If the watch is bigger than your head, it's too big. Actually, it should never be bigger than a half dollar.

CUFF LINKS

In the last few years, there's been a subtle shift in men's fashion. Because a lot of guys aren't wearing suits—or even ties—every day, the shirt itself has now become the canvas for self-expression. Everywhere you look, you see beautiful striped woven shirts that look cool whether you wear them with dress slacks or with denim.

With great thanks to our friends across the pond, a lot of the wonderful shirts out there, from Thomas Pink to Paul Smith to moderate American designers, now have French cuffs. And American men are baffled by them. They leave the cuffs hanging all the way down to their fingertips or they roll them up. Wrong answer. By doing that, you're not making the most of what can be a great look—all it takes is a simple investment in a great pair of cuff links. Don't be afraid.

Adding cuff links can really personalize your wardrobe. They can say a lot about your personality and add a lot of sass or class. They can act as a nod to a favorite hobby, a zodiac sign, whatever. They shouldn't be too big and you should avoid being too whimsical: Teddy bears and bunny rabbits might not be the best choice for attracting a mate.

For a classic look, I love a nice sterling silver oval from Tiffany. If you want to do something funky or fun, and you don't want to spend a lot of money, flea markets and secondhand stores offer an amazing array of cuff links for next to nothing. Problem solved!

SUNGLASSES

I can't say enough about the importance of sunglasses. They protect your eyes, keep you from squinting, and prevent the need for Botox in the future. *And* they make you look like a movie star. What more do you want? It's the easiest fix in the

without sunglasses

with sunglasses

book. When I put a great pair of sunglasses on somebody, it's *always* transforming.

You've now heard me say this a million times, but when looking for sunglasses, keep it simple. If you go crazy with sunglasses, you'll look like Elton John or somebody from MTV's *House of Style* or like you just got back from Ibiza. We don't want that. No colored tints, either, or you'll risk looking like Anastacia. I love her music, but it's not the right look for most men. Bone structure. Go figure. You want classic sunglasses, like Ray-Ban Wayfarers, which Tom Cruise wore in *Risky Business*. Aviators also look hot on almost everybody. (Hello! Tom Cruise in *Top Gun*!) In fact, when in doubt, just try to look like Tom Cruise.

Sunglasses are artwork that frames your face. And, um, hi?! It's your face! Take it seriously. You want to be concerned about scale and fit, and make sure that the frames balance out your face. If you're fair with pale hair, a black frame might be too severe. Try a tortoise in softer, warmer brown or gold tones. For dark hair, silver is an excellent choice.

We all know that you can find really cheap sunglasses on the street or at the dollar store. And that can sometimes be appealing because a lot of us tend to lose them, sit on them, whatever, and we don't want to make a big investment. But I think quality is very important when it comes to sunglasses, so it might be worth it to spend just a little more. Proceed with caution when purchasing sunglasses at a place that also sells hemorrhoid ointment, because we're talking about your eyes here. Make sure that whatever you buy is UV resistant. If you doubt how important that is, let me just remind you that German shepherds are expensive. So are canes. And just imagine never being able to indulge in the visual pleasure of your next visit to Hooters.

EYEGLASSES

In this era of laser eye surgery and disposable contact lenses, don't forget that glasses can be hot and very sexy. They're not just for geeks anymore. People do make passes at guys who wear glasses. Trust me.

When choosing a pair of glasses—or maybe while complaining about how expensive they can be—remember one thing: You should never slap just anything on your face. You're not welding here, people. You're going to be walking around all day and night with these glasses on. It's the one accessory that stays with you all the time, which makes glasses probably the most important thing you have in your wardrobe.

I trust you're working with a top-quality optometrist who will ensure the safety of your peepers. Beyond that, glasses are a fashion item, subject to old domestic partner tales à la "Pleated pants will hide my spare tire." People fall prey to believing things like "I'll wear glasses with clear frames. They'll recede from my face and it will look like I'm not wearing glasses at all!" Here's the snafu: The rest of us aren't blind. We know you're wearing glasses. And clear frames went out with earth shoes, okay?

It's always best to buy a simple frame that flatters you. Avoid any kind of fashion frames. You don't want to look like Sally Jessy Raphael. There are some classic frames that always look great on everybody—preppy styles and simple wire frames are always good choices. A sleek but still classic option is the rimless frame. A total oxymoron, but doable nonetheless.

Just like sunglasses, pick your glasses carefully. Do they fit your face? Do they flatter you? Do they balance your look? Are they too big? Too small? Made of good materials? Do they work with your coloring? Do they make your butt look huge?

As with everything else in your wardrobe, you need to buy new glasses every couple of years or so. You buy new shoes and new clothes from time to time, so why would you keep wearing glasses from 1984? If you can afford it, why not get two pairs? That way you can switch up your look and always keep it fresh.

I always say you should never shop alone, but that's particularly true when you're investing in something as important as eyewear. It can cost hundreds of dollars, and it's framing your most important feature. Okay, well maybe your second most important. Faces are overrated. Nonetheless you should have someone there to give you a second opinion, because you can't see everything accurately. Here's my Mr. Wizard science lesson for today: When you look at something in the mirror, you're getting a two-dimensional image. But you're a three-dimensional person, so the way things look in a mirror is not always the way they look to other people. And voilà. That's where your trusty second opinion comes in.

BELTS

I hesitated to even include belts with accessories, lest you underestimate their importance and think of them as optional. Belts are not accessories in the truest sense of that word. Belts are *requirements*, people. You should probably be wearing a belt about 90 percent of the time. Have at least one for every day of the week—just as long as they don't *say* the names of the days of the week on them.

Why are belts so important? Well, I always like to say that personality starts in the crotch region, and why not draw attention to it by wearing a fantastic belt? Since men wear so few accessories, a belt can say so much about you and add flair to otherwise boring looks. Even if you only have one or two great leather straps, they're versatile. Change out the buckles, and get that much more use out of them.

A bad belt, on the other hand, is like a bad pair of shoes—you can spot poor quality a mile away. If your belt is vinyl or vegetarian leather with a cheap aluminum buckle, people can tell. They notice that you're not paying attention to detail. They might not even realize it consciously, but in the back of their minds, they'll see you and think, "Hmmmm. Something just isn't right here. There's big trouble in River City."

Heather has two mommies . . . and you should have two different types of belts: dressy and casual. Generally speaking, skinnier belts are dressier, meant for suits and dressed-up sportswear, while chunkier, thicker belts are for wearing with casual pants—denim, cargo, roughwear, corduroys.

The belts that you wear with a suit should be sleek and simple. The whole point of wearing a suit is having a sophisticated, luxurious uniform that's about understate-

Is Your Belt Buckle Too Big?

If you look like an Oklahoma State team roping champion, like you've won a major prizefight, or if you risk injury when sitting, your buckle is too big.

Bigger than a quarter? Okay.

Bigger than a cookie? Still okay.

A 9-volt battery? Sure.

Bar of soap? Risky.

A piece of toast? Too big.

CD? Do I really need to go there?

And yet again, your head? Seek counseling.

ment and elegance. The belt you wear should add to that feeling. This is where you should invest in a couple of great pieces like a crocodile strap and an engine-turned buckle. Diminutive hardware in nickel, sterling, or unpolished brass on a simple leather or alligator strap is always best. These really are investments, so don't balk at spending a little more for quality. The classic styles don't change too much with the times, so if you invest in a couple of good ones now, you'll have them for the rest of your life.

Casual belts are where you can really have fun. There's a great selection of cool casual belts available in leather, nylon, grosgrain, etc. I love old western belts and buckles or those with cool logos or your name on them. They look fantastic with denim. And you can throw in some whimsical ribbon belts for summer. You can also find cool military-inspired vintage belts at thrift stores, vintage shops, or army surplus stores.

Just for the record, you may have seen me wear a belt with a pair of pants that didn't actually have belt loops—say, sweatpants. That is definitely not for amateurs. Do as I say, not as I do. There are some things Mother just can't explain.

aka BRACES

SUSPENDERS

This will be admittedly brief. Who really wears suspenders anymore? The Amish, yes. Really weird people with no lives who attend *Mork and Mindy* conventions, yes. Most sane people, no.

I do think suspenders are so cool, though. They look really sophisticated with a suit or a tuxedo. (And by the way—you're buying that tuxedo, not renting, right? See chapter nine.) Suspenders should be made of silk, grosgrain, or fine cotton webbing, but they can also be made of braided leather. With a finely tailored suit where the pants are constructed with side tabs and no belt loops, they add a certain Wall Street panache. I think of Michael Douglas as Gordon Gekko. Since you don't see them too often, I think they make for a really special look.

Suspenders should never be worn with anything else but a suit or a tuxedo. Otherwise it's way too *What's Happening!!* Never wear a belt when you wear suspenders, and for God's sake, don't clip them on to jeans.

BAGS

Just like all of your other accessories, the bags you use to haul your stuff around in can add a lot of flair and personality to your look. Here are a few basic bags you shouldn't be without.

1. **The "man bag" or "murse." Most guys carry a lot of stuff to and from work, including a laptop and files. You don't want to carry it around in ShopRite bags or you'll look like a homeless person. You need a good-looking carryall. Not Kitty Carryall, doll.**

   My favorite everyday bag is a suede or leather messenger bag. It has enough room for your laptop, your files, and some other day-to-day necessities. (You probably already have a desk and an office, or cargo pants, so it shouldn't be *too* huge. Carrying it shouldn't give you a herniated disk.) There are also some cool nylon varieties out there by companies like Jack Spade. You just have to be careful with nylon because it can look like it's from the IBM collection. They make great computers, but they're not so great with fashion.

I know, I know. You're going to tell me that bags actually designed as computer bags are better for your computer. But they don't look good! If it came with your computer or from an office supply store, just throw it away. Or save it and give it to someone you don't like for the holidays. Sometimes you have to be a slave to fashion, people. So what if you lose all your data from having your laptop jostled around? There could be worse things. Like being heckled on the commuter train.

You might be the rare and lucky recipient of a bag actually designed to hold a computer that also actually looks good. But odds are it might cost more than your laptop. Avoid bags that cost more than the computer you're carrying in them. Or just trust me and stick with the messenger bag, okay?

Now, every once in a while, I come across a straight guy who insists on carrying a "man purse," which is any bag that's smaller than a laptop bag, a gym bag, or a satchel, but bigger than a wallet. These are treacherous waters, people. Carrying a leather man purse can make you look like Mackenzie Phillips on *One Day at a Time* if you're not careful. Even if it's a little bigger than you need and you don't have enough stuff to fill it up, I still recommend a leather messenger bag rather than a man purse. So much more masculine. Fill it with porn for all I care, just put something in there.

2. The athletic or gym bag. If you're going to carry your gym bag to and from work every day, please don't let it be one you got free with a bottle of cologne, a deposit at your bank, or your tenth oil change at Jiffy Lube. The giveaway bag is like the free T-shirt. It's free! So there's a reason it looks that way. Just store it in a box marked "yard sale." A gym bag should be stylish—something sleek, black, and nylon, with logos kept to a minimum. Carrying a dumpy free bag is just like putting a bad raincoat over a great look. It's a buzzkill. It can ruin National Coming Out Day for everyone!

3. The weekender bag. In this day and age, most people aren't going on really long vacations; they're taking shorter trips and weekend getaways. And while it saddens me that the Louis Vuitton steamer trunk has gone the way of the Edsel, that means that you'll need a good weekend bag.

You should also invest in a good quality leather or nylon dopp kit, either to take to the gym or on vacation. I keep mine packed all the time with my cleanser, toner, moisturizer, toothbrush, deodorant, laminated photos of Cher, etc. That way, I have all my basics ready to go at all times and I never forget something when I go on a trip. The dopp kit can be pretty compact; it doesn't have to be big enough to fit a giant can of Rave hairspray. Because hairspray—the product, not the musical, that is—is never the right answer.

Personally, I think a leather duffel is the perfect thing to hold a weekend's worth of clothes. It's good-looking, handsome, and classic, just like a Baldwin! And it will get better with age, unlike your sex life.

A leather duffel doesn't need to be made by an expensive designer; just be sure to look for good quality leather, stitching, and overall construction. It should be roomy, and ideally will have a nice silk or rayon lining. Don't get crazy and demand all sorts of pockets and pouches. They're like bad wedding gifts; you never use them.

LUGGAGE OR EMOTIONAL BAGGAGE

There's nothing sadder than noticing a hot guy at the airport and then seeing him retrieve a bag from the carousel that's covered with teal and lime green oversized tapestry flowers straight from the Cindy Brady collection. Handsome luggage is important. I'm not sure why the worst dressed people in the world are always at the airport. Just don't be one of them. You're traveling, not cleaning out your basement or getting an MRI.

Good luggage can be expensive, but remember you're probably never going to go on safari for a month, so your luggage needs are actually pretty modest. Register for it when you get married! Or just invest in one good quality suitcase and one high-quality garment bag with lots of storage compartments. If you also have a leather weekend bag, you really don't need much more. When shopping for luggage, keep in mind that larger items that need to be checked through your friendly airport baggage handling system might not receive the greatest of care, and should be as durable as possible. Remember the American Tourister gorilla? You should be so lucky.

What to Pack for a Weekend Away

a pair of jeans

a couple of white T-shirts

a blazer

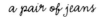

a couple pairs of
clean underwear

a couple
pairs of
black
socks

plain white athletic socks

athletic shoes

a ballcap

a pair of nylon swim
trunks (you can run
in them, work out in
them, or swim if the
hotel has a pool)

a blue
oxford
shirt

a pair of
driving mocs

one great belt that matches the driving mocs

a cashmere sweater
(dressy and casual
covered in one swoop)

Wallets: Is That a Wallet in Your Pocket, or Are You Just Happy to See Me?

Personally, I like to see guys with a big bulge in the front and not in the back. And if you sit on a bulging wallet all day, it can lead to back problems and other strains: total chiropractic moment. You also shouldn't keep a big bulky wallet in the breast pocket of your jacket because it will make you look like you have lopsided gynecomastia.

A big overstuffed wallet is a liability in any case, because if you keep everything that's important to you in there, you're so out of luck should you lose it or become the victim of a pickpocket. All of your favorite pictures of your dog, your high school girlfriend's graduation picture, and the ones of hot frat boys you've downloaded from the Internet would all be gone, as would your credit cards and other important personal documents.

Keep your wallet sleek and small and keep the rest of your important items at home in a safe place. Personally, I keep a nice simple little wallet that has a bit of room for my driver's license, two or three credit cards, and a few dead presidents. Cash is so vintage.

I don't think it's even that crucial to have a matched set of luggage; great-looking pieces that look better on their own are more important. How often do you really run around carrying all of your luggage at once? Unless you're costarring with Bette Davis in some 1930s movie about star-crossed lovers and ocean travel, you should be fine.

Modern luggage is not only great because it looks good, but because it has this amazing feature: I don't know if they're new, but they're called "wheels." I'm always amazed that there are people who still haven't caught on to the wheeled luggage phenomenon and are carting around old buckled suitcases with huge Naugahyde handles that look like they came from the Sanford and Son's estate sale. Hernias are *so* not cute. Also keep in mind that if there's duct tape anywhere on it, or it needs to be closed with the help of a bungee cord or strap, it should be tossed.

Pack Your Bags!
A Carson How To . . .

Packing your suitcase is like making lasagna. It's all about the layers. You want your bag to be bottom heavy, so your shoes should always go in first, along with any other heavy or bulky items. I'm a big fan of tucking things inside my shoes—eyewear, socks, anything little like that. It's space-saving and also acts to insulate and protect those items. In between the shoes, I stuff things that you don't really have to worry about getting wrinkled, like underwear.

Your next layer will be blazers, pants, and sweaters. You don't want to fold anything harshly because that will leave a hard crease. A great trick is to take a garment like a blazer, put it in a dry-cleaning bag and tie the bag at the bottom so you're creating a pillow of air around it. Roll it and voilà! Next come your sweaters, which should also be gently folded and rolled. This is probably not for amateurs, but if you have the time, layer your sweaters in tissue paper before you pack them. That's why nicer stores use tissue when you buy something; it supports without wrinkling.

The top layer of your bag will be your woven shirts, because they're the most delicate and the most subject to getting crushed. Again, these can be wrapped in tissue to help prevent wrinkling. Or, more realistically, you can just send them out when you get to the hotel, and they'll come back all fresh and lovely. If the idea of spending $10 to press a shirt while you're on the road gives you pause, fear not. Unless you're staying at a motel where they charge by the hour, there should be an iron in your room—or you can usually call housekeeping and request one. If you're absolutely stuck somewhere without an iron, or short on time, hang your shirt in the bathroom and run a hot shower—the steam will eliminate the wrinkles.

Your toiletries should always be in a separate compartment from your clothes. I learned that the hard way, when my purple Paul Mitchell color-protecting shampoo leaked out onto one of my favorite yellow cashmere sweaters. It was one of life's very hard lessons, but I hope to spare you a similar fate.

You can also protect against such tragedies by keeping anything that could leak in a Ziploc bag and/or wrapping your garments in plastic bags. As a bonus, it's also a good idea in the unlikely event of a water landing!

Always the Wrong Answer . . .

Puka shell necklaces. Unless you're one of the Beach Boys or your career aspirations are to be a host at a Polynesian restaurant, leave your puka shells with your inhibitions at the beach, okay?

Cell phones on belts. Never, ever.

Keys on chains clipped to your belt. Not unless you're a janitor or a prison warden (both of which happen to be hot).

Wallets on chains. Not unless you're a Hell's Angel, in which case let me give you my number.

Skin art. I love a hot tattoo, but it should be like the prize at the bottom of the Cracker Jack box: Your "friend" should discover it. Those of you with Vanilla Ice tattoos on your forearm will agree.

Gold teeth. For rappers only.

Rainbow suspenders. Three words: Mork from Ork. Actually, rainbow anything is always the wrong answer. I hope that doesn't alienate me from my gay brethren, but really! No more freedom rings. The flag is plenty, people.

Eyeglasses with decal stickers of your initials. Sooo very Linda Richman.

Techno eyeglasses that look like pieces of German drafting equipment.

Fanny packs. Puh-leeze.

Backpacks. Your life is not an episode of 90210, and you're not hiking the Alps every day. They're just a little juvenile. But if you also carry a *Rugrats* lunchbox, then they're fine.

8

The Eighties Called, They Want Your Hair Back

SKIN, HAIR, AND NAILS, AND OTHER REASONS WHY YOU SHOULD DRINK MILK

YOU CAN BE THE BEST-DRESSED GUY ON THE PLANET—AND IF YOU'VE GOTTEN THIS FAR IN THE BOOK, YOU WILL BE!—BUT IF YOU'VE got horrendo breath, ratty hair, and nails that look like Grandpa Munster's, you're in big trouble. Here's how to make sure that doesn't happen.

HAIR

If I may quote Elle Woods in *Legally Blonde* (perhaps the finest cinematographic work of art ever created), "The rules of hair care are simple and finite." Your hair is your **crowning glory**. Whether you have a ton of it or just three or four strands, you should take care that it looks well groomed. Why? Because life is too short to have bad hair. I always say you shouldn't leave the house unless your hair is perfect or close to it. Tardy, schmardy.

In order to have great hair, you need a great stylist. You should take as much care in finding the right hairstylist as you would in selecting a doctor. It's that important. Good haircuts do cost more money because these people are trained professionals. The good news is you don't have to spend a million dollars on your hair every time you get it cut. But once or twice a year, go to an excellent salon and get a really great cut from a true hair care professional—or HCP, if you will.

A lot of men are guilty of overwashing their hair, especially if you're an active guy going to the gym a lot. Shower daily, please, by all means. That's fine. But you don't have to use shampoo every day. Every third day don't use shampoo, just use conditioner. It will allow some of that natural oil to accumulate. You know why mink looks so great? Because the fur is brimming with natural oils. When you wash your hair too much, you strip all that away. Big faux paws. I mean pas.

Now here's the trick: In between visits to your HCP, you can go to a good quality barber for haircuts. As long as you don't have a really tricky haircut, a barber can maintain the shape and texture of the haircut created by your HCP.

When you find the right cut for you, it will appear very natural. If you have curly hair, embrace the curl, don't fight it. If you have straight hair, do the same. Find the cut that naturally makes you look your best. And don't forget to maintain it. You really need to go about every five weeks for maintenance. Otherwise it's just going to lose its shape and start to look sloppy.

Product: The Final Frontier

The hair care aisle at your local drugstore, supermarket, or high-end beauty supply boutique is treacherous territory, even for those who've been through the rigors of beauty school. There's a reason so many men fear hair products. Too much of them is a bad thing. But products are out there because they help people. I don't know how we lived without them. I ask myself this question often. Looking at photos from the days of yore, I ponder, "How *did* they do that without the benefit of gels, creams, and foaming pomades?"

Anyway, it's very easy to find the right products: Just leave this one to your HCP, who can steer you depending on the texture, cut, weight, density, etc., of your hair. Everyone's hair is so very different that I can't make one sweeping generalization or recommend any specific line or brand. So trust in your HCP to set up a hair care regimen (henceforth known as HCR) specially designed just for you.

Losing Your Hair: On Your Head, Not So Good. On Your Back, That's a Different Story Entirely.

It's just a sad fact of being a man that some of us draw the short stick in the genetic lottery and lose our hair. But with hair, as with just about everything but penis size, it's all about quality not quantity. If you find yourself losing your hair, just get a good cut and go with it.

I can't endorse any of the common "fixes" to going bald. That bushy Krusty the Clown do with tufts on either side? You end

COMBOVER

(before)

TOUPEE

(before)

up looking like Princess Leia or like you have earmuffs on all the time. Please don't fall victim to the lure of the combover. Combovers make me want to scream, "Hi! Your reality check bounced! You're not fooling anyone!" You'll look like "The Donald" with "The combover." And as a general rule you don't want to look like anybody with "the" in front of their name. Think about it. The Grinch. The Hamburgler. The Joker. I rest my (attaché) case.

(after)

And whatever you do, do not let me catch you wearing a rug. Rugs are for floors. Toupee, shmoupee: It's a wig. And wigs are just not an option. Besides, bald guys are hot. Think Telly Savalas. Hot! Bruce Willis. Hotter! Vin Diesel. Don't get me started.

(after)

If your hair is thinning and it's dark, a nice little trick is to get a few highlights. Please don't fear the highlights. But don't overdo them either. Too many highlights in short hair can make you look like a leopard. Way too Discovery Channel.

If you're trying to avoid gray, I say, embrace it. Go with it. Don't try to cover it up. Inevitably when you try to cover it, you get that color that's too uniform and dark. You know, it's always the color of the top of a cob of corn—that rusty brown. It makes you look like you have pubic hair on your head. Damn you, Ron Popeil! So just work with it. Think of your gray as a mark of being distinguished and having great life experiences. Salt and pepper's hot. That's the hair color, not the band.

FACIAL HAIR

I love a little facial hair. Actually, I'd love to be able to grow some. But the hair on your face is just like the hair on your head: It needs to be well kept and well managed. You don't want to look like Abe Lincoln, Grizzly Adams, or like you own an Amish roadside vegetable stand. You also don't want to exfoliate your partner every time you make out, or transmit little mites from your scabie-licious stubble. Ahhh, scabies. Has there ever been a skin disorder so appropriately named?

If you're wondering about how much or how little facial hair can work for you, speak to that fabulous HCP of yours. Well-groomed facial hair can actually cover up some facial flaws or accentuate your better features. You can use sideburns to create more of a cheekbone, for instance. It's very personal, and a good stylist can help make it work for you.

When it comes to shaving, I only have one piece of advice: Take your time! It's not a race. Let's take a moment to think about the physics of shaving. Hmmmm. Razor-sharp blade right next to your jugular. So let's not be hasty, shall we?

As for shaving cream, I think it's all about quality. Some higher-end products are simply better, in my opinion. They're made from natural products like lanolin or aloe vera. Natural is almost always better. If you doubt it, riddle me this: When's the last time you slept with a trannie? But there are exceptions. If you have an inexpensive drugstore brand that works with your skin, that's great. Shaving is about getting it to stand up, lubricating it, and then stroking gently. "It" means your facial hair, but this is a process with which I'm sure you're well acquainted.

. . . OR "MANSCAPING"

BODY HAIR

Once you've dealt with the hair on your head and your face, I recommend you use a nose hair clipper to get rid of any additional hair coming out of orifices or pores, whether it's the ear, nose, or ass crack. As for the brows, I don't want to see them plucked and tweezed like Joan Crawford's. They don't have to be perfectly formed. They shouldn't be shaved. They just shouldn't be connected all the way across like a Bering Strait you can walk right over. Waxing can be your friend. Don't be afraid.

And now we get to my least favorite, the hairy back. A little bit of hair back there is not the end of the world, but if you're at the beach and people are complimenting you on your sweater and you're not wearing one, we've got a back hair situation, people. I call this profusion of body hair "Mangora." You could shave it, but this would require a partner. What are you doing Tuesdays at eleven? Right after your favorite show ends on Bravo? Otherwise, just get thee to a waxer. Pronto.

THE SKIN YOU'RE IN

There's a reason women age better than their husbands. It's because they know how important it is to take care of their skin. Since many men work in grueling physical environments like extreme heat, cold, or sun, all preventive measures must be taken to protect your favorite organ . . . your skin. Did you know that your skin is the largest organ of your body? It is. Don't flatter yourself.

I don't know why so many men neglect their skin care. Hello! It's your face. And it's really okay these days to care about your skin. It's just like taking care of your car. You wash it, you buff it, you wax it—otherwise known as cleanse, exfoliate, and moisturize.

Why cleanse? Because there's tons and tons of grime and buildup that accumulate in your pores as you go about your daily routine. You're exposed to outside pollutants, city dirt and grime, and natural oils. A good test for that: If your pillow is dirty, you've probably got dirty skin. Or you're into some kinky bedroom fantasies I don't even want to know about.

You basically want to keep the skin clean, but you don't want to strip it or scrub it down to the bone. So you use a mild cleanser formulated for your skin type: oily, dry, or combination. I recommend cleansing as part of your morning routine and then again when you go to bed, to remove that full day's buildup. To keep it simple, keep your facial cleanser in the shower, so you don't need to add an extra step to your daily routine. And besides, it's fun taking care of business in the shower.

Exfoliation is the part where you gently scrub away the dead skin cells. Exfoliate once a week and you're golden, pony boy. On Saturdays, while in between college football games, why not live large and exfoliate?

Moisturizing is like putting that final protective coat of wax on your car. Moisturizers keep the skin soft and conditioned. They should be rich in natural antioxidants, but they shouldn't make you break out. Acne was sad at thirteen; it's tragic at thirty-three. Don't fear that moisturizers are too girly. There's a full array of men's

Everyone looks good with a healthy glow. But we all know we need to stay out of the sun and use a good quality sunscreen with a high SPF every day of the year. There are a plethora of sunless tanning gels and creams on the market that can give you a healthy glow without landing you at Sloan Kettering. No one wants to look like Magda, the frighteningly leather-skinned neighbor from *There's Something About Mary.*

Just make sure you use the right products for the right part of your body. Your body needs a different product from your face because the texture and sensitivity of the skin on your face is different from the skin on your body.

moisturizers that are unscented. You can find them in drugstores or department stores. You don't have to make an appointment with your mother's Mary Kay lady.

When it comes to finding the right products for your skin, there are some drugstore brands—Neutrogena and ROC come to mind—that are good products that won't clog your cute little pores. But I do think it's smart to take a little more care and consider going to a department store, specialty apothecary, or skin care center. There's no shame in going to the beauty counter and asking for help. It's not some terrible sin like wearing white after Labor Day. Odds are a very hot sales associate will direct you to the men's skin care area, which, much like the population of China, seems to be getting bigger every day.

For the ultimate in skin care, I highly recommend that every man get a facial twice a year. It's just like cleaning your teeth or changing your oil. You do that, don't ya?

How to find a facialist? Ask around. Ask your girlfriend, your mom, your gay lover. I mean uncle. Ask that coworker of yours who's so fond of the *Funny Girl* soundtrack. Or even easier, when you're seeing your HCP, ask if the salon has a facialist. If they don't, just ask your HCP if he or she can suggest one. Hairdressers just know these kinds of things. And just like your hair care professional, your facialist can advise you on what skin care products you should be using to keep it (and you) looking its best.

NAILS

If you're going to be holding hands with your girl, there's nothing worse than big old mangled man hands. Clean fingernails are of the utmost importance. No woman wants to hold your hand if it has enough dirt on it to pot a geranium.

So let's put the "man" back in "manicure," shall we? It's not called a "ladycure," now, is it? It's a very simple procedure in which no straight people are hurt, I promise. Manicures are a really inexpensive treat—between $10 and $15 for a nice little hand job! Sometimes it's a real pick-me-up. Odds are there will be a cute Asian girl named Kim who weighs less than your head performing the procedure—bonus!

There's no polish involved if that's what frightens you, as it does *moi*. They'll just clean you up and fix all those ragged cuticles. You can get a simple buff on your nails, which is just like buffing your car: It's a little low abrasion that makes them smooth and even and gives a very matte shine. Or you can just go au naturel.

Taking care of your toenails is important, too, especially during the summer, or if you share your bed with anyone. Your toenails should not be weapons or the star of a new television series called *When Toenails Attack*.

I'm also a big fan of the pedicure, which is all about getting your hooves in good order, as we say in the horse industry. No hoof, no horse. Again, there's no need to fear that getting a pedicure means painting your toenails; a good pedicurist is just going to clean up your feet, which is a beautiful thing.

I know that regular pedicures are not for everyone, and we've got to do this in baby steps—pun intended. In fact, the idea of walking into a nail salon for a pedicure is just too scary for many straight men. And that's okay; just promise me you'll clip those toenails at home in the privacy of your own woodworking shop. But if you're going on vacation, you might want to consider indulging in a pedicure. Cross over to the dark side. Follow me. You might never go back.

SCENT OF A MAN

THE While some members of my community may enjoy the smell of a musky bear, most people do not. So unless you're planning on moving to France, I recommend you invest in a good quality deodorant. But let's not forget to protect our clothing friends, shall we? Use a deodorant that doesn't stain or ruin your undergarments or dress shirts. That would be like cutting off your nose to spite your face—or like throwing out your Pradas to spite your Guccis.

When it comes to deodorants, keep it simple. It's all about being fresh and clean. I would avoid scents in your deodorants and save that for your cologne. I actually feel the same way about soap. Showering once a day won't kill you, but I like an unscented soap, and one that's non-comedogenic, so it won't clog the pores on your ass cheeks. I don't like guys who smell like bars of soap or have pimples on their butts. Call me crazy!

As for fragrance, a man with a little—and remember I said "a little"—scent on is hot. It's sexy and yummy and lovely, and the ladies love it. I'm not talking about the scent of musty underwear or an old gym sock, by the way, I'm talking about cologne. Cologne should always be subtle and never overwhelming. Put on far less than you think you would need. A great way to apply cologne is to spray it in front of you and then walk through the mist rather than applying it directly. That will keep your fellow elevator passengers from thinking you bathed in a vat of Paco Rabanne. That's always the wrong answer.

It would be impossible for me to tell you how to buy cologne. Choosing a fragrance is so very personal. There are millions of options out there, and you just need

Great style starts with a white smile. Life's just too short to have yellow teeth, so I suggest you try a whitening product. There's a multitude of products on the market that you can now get at any drugstore. And yes, they really work.

138 OFF THE CUFF

to experiment and use a little common sense. If it's called "Eau de Farm Animal," or the bottle has a guarantee that it will improve your sex life, you might want to think again. Take a lady friend with you and try on a couple different scents.

I'll also warn you that if you like a scent someone has on, feel free to ask him about it, but keep in mind that a scent on one person is not going to necessarily smell the same on someone else, because of body chemistry and body oils and whatnot.

9

WHO WEARS WHAT, WHEN, WHY, AND HOW

HERE'S WHERE I'LL SHOW YOU HOW TO DRESS APPROPRIATELY FOR YOUR **A**GE, THE **S**ETTING, AND THE **S**EASON (AKA ASS) . . . IN OTHER words, how to keep from looking like a complete ass.

FOR YOUR AGE

DRESSING

Imagine this. Would you like to see your mom in a tube top? No. I didn't think so. Which is why it's so important to look right for who you are.

That means if you're thirty-four, it's time to throw out your college sweats and T-shirts. There are other joys right around the corner that don't involve kegs, I promise. I don't like seeing forty-year-old guys wearing Abercrombie & Fitch. I also don't like to see young guys wearing

fashion amnesia

dress your age

bow ties and sweater vests. And if you're sixty-five, you probably don't want to be wearing the latest bikini swimsuit from the International Male catalog. You want to dress your age, not your shoe size.

The moral of the story is that there's a right look for every age, and you should enjoy each phase of your life and not try to live in another one. Don't try to look older or younger than you actually are. Embrace where you are and enjoy it. Savor the moment. Carpe diem, people!

The problem is that guys get stuck in a rut. They have a moment in time when they think they looked the best and will just keep wearing the clothes from that era. It's called fashion amnesia. They'll decide, for example, that they looked phat when they graduated from college, and so they get locked into that style. That's why you'll see these modern-day Rip Van Winkles sporting keyboard ties and parachute pants. You're like, "Hi! *Saved By the Bell* is long over. You might think you look good, but dude, you're forty now. Looking like Screech is not going to work anymore. Maybe that's why you're still dateless in Seattle."

Everything in your closet should have an expiration date on it, just the way milk, bread, magazines, and newspapers do. I've found that men tend to keep absolutely everything in their closets. And if you tell them to get rid of it, they insist that they "might wear that!" I say, "Really? Are you going back to high school graduation again? Are you going to keep that cap and gown?"

I'm not saying you should look like you just stepped out of the pages of *L'Uomo Vogue*, because most guys can't pull that off. And if you can, I'll want to pull it off, as in, "Pull that off! Now!" You've just got to remember to update. Find a classic, timeless style that works for you and doesn't make you look like you're a tour guide at Colonial Williamsburg.

It all comes down to not pretending to be something that you're not. Speaking of which, let me say again that I don't want anyone reading this book to emulate me, although I know how tempting it is. I want you to look like yourself and no one else. Think of it as a celebration of you if you will; a real "you-fest" or "all-about-you-palooza."

FOR THE SETTING

DRESSING

Sure, it's fun to be expressive and bend the fashion rules, because the first rule is that there are no rules. There are a lot of times you want to stand out and be an individual, but there are also times when the occasion dictates a quiet elegance or sobriety. You want to show off your personal style, but you don't want to stick out like a sore thumb. At weddings, funerals, job interviews, IPOs, bar mitzvahs, the Oscars, and divorce court, you want to dress up and show respect. You'll most likely be meeting people you have never seen before in your life. So, bottom line? You don't want to look like a boob. Win them over with your great personality, not your "vintage" Dockers.

It's all about appropriateness. And there's absolutely nothing harder to explain than what is considered appropriate. It's kind of like Supreme Court Justice Potter Stewart's comment on pornography: "I know it when I see it." But there are some general guidelines you can keep in mind.

Do your homework. Find out about the occasion or event so you can dress appropriately. You're a reporter now. Ask some questions. Take some notes. Practice the "six p's": Proper planning prevents poor performance, people.

Life is like theater—it's one big musical and you have to look the part. Who are your castmates and what's the set like? (Relax. I think I'm done with the musical theater metaphors for now.) Is it cocktails at the country club with Muffy and Tripp or a low-key hoedown and tractor pull? Sometimes you have to wear a costume. And believe me, I know. This isn't my first day at the gay rodeo.

The best rule of thumb I can give you is that it's always better to be over-dressed than underdressed. If you're not sure if the event requires a tie, bring one with you and scope out the scene. You can always put the tie on if it's required, or leave it in your pocket, bag, or glove compartment if it's not. Not having a tie in a situation where one is called for is bad news. It's like showing up at a black tie wedding in a suit or at a job interview in sweatpants.

If you're on a date or you're proposing to someone, you want to show you care. Make an effort. If you're going to church, dress up a little. It's God's house, people.

If you're a guest at a wedding, it's about respecting someone's special day. If I may paraphrase Sergio Valente, how you look on the outside tells the world how you feel on the inside.

Work Situations

Job interviews are a fashion no-brainer, people. You wear a suit to a job interview unless you're interviewing with the department of sanitation. No shame in that game, by the way, but you just won't need a suit. And as we learned in chapter five, unless you're something like the Nell character from the Jodie Foster movie, you will own one good quality suit for just such an occasion.

When it comes to the workplace, one of my peeps says you always want to dress for the job that you want, not the job you have. Dressing below your job rank will only make people in your human resources department question themselves: "Hmmm. Look at those pleated khakis and that Muppets tie. Is Bob really CEO material? Maybe he'd be better in the mailroom."

Now, if you work in the kind of environment where you would get laughed at for wearing a suit, that doesn't mean you should come in wearing gym clothes for that big presentation. There is such a thing as high-quality casual clothing. How about a V-neck merino sweater, a crisp white shirt, flat-front dress trousers, a beautiful belt, and a great-looking watch? People will think, "He looks great and has really taken the time to prepare for this." Well-constructed garments don't have to look dressy to look sophisticated. Call it casual power dressing.

Black Tie

Nothing strikes as much fear into the average guy's heart as being invited to a black tie event. Well, nothing except impotence, that is. Relax. Not many of us have the opportunity to wear formal wear very often. It's really just for very special occasions. Unless you're a debutante (in which case I'm jealous) or an executive at a Fortune 500 company, your social calendar is unlikely to be chock-full of black tie events. But the occasional black tie wedding or benefit does fall into many men's lives, so you might as well be prepared.

The funny thing is that formal wear is probably the least frightening of all fashion situations because you really don't have too many choices or options. It's almost like a uniform. It's as easy as black and white. Here, more than anywhere, I urge you to remember: Keep it simple, sister. If you are not someone who needs more than one formal outfit, buy yourself one classic black tuxedo with a peaked lapel jacket. Look no further. Nothing makes you look more like a movie star.

Notice how I said *buy* yourself a tuxedo, not *rent* yourself a tuxedo? I know, you're frightened. You're lost. But a rented tuxedo is the worst thing I can think of other than nuclear holocaust. That thing is caked in DNA, trust me. Do you know how many proms it's been to? It's a vessel, a conduit if you will, for the aromas of all former wearers. I suggest you visit a discount clothier and drop the $500 to $1000 for a quality tuxedo instead. Even if you go to only five formal events in your entire lifetime, it will have almost paid for itself. And there's really no price you can put on looking that much cooler.

If renting is really your only option, you should rent only what I'm about to prescribe: a very classic tuxedo in simple black and white. Don't let them talk you into the matching lavender cummerbund and bow tie. Before you know you'll be into show tunes.

So here's what a classic tux looks like from top to bottom. It's very, very, *very* simple. We start with that classic peaked lapel jacket in black, right?

THE TUXEDO SHIRT should be a white shirt with a simple point collar, not a wing tip or you'll look like a bartender on the Love Boat. Do I even need to say it doesn't have ruffles?

I also hear that there is a vast conspiracy in the wedding industry to force grooms to wear ivory tux shirts if their brides are wearing ivory dresses, in order to keep those ivory gowns from appearing "dirty" by contrast. And while our friends in the rental tuxedo industry might really have your best interests in mind, this is ridiculous. Black

Holiday Dressing

My rule on this is simple: Turkeys and hams should dress for the holidays. People shouldn't.

At holiday time, it's all about rich colors and rich fabrics like velvets and cashmere. It's not about blinking reindeer noses and Be-Dazzled candy canes. When in doubt, dress like a normal person at the holidays and not someone on their break from Trudee's Kraft Korrall.

tie is about black and white and no other colors. Period. You are never going to see enough of the shirt to cause a clash, and besides, you're a bride and groom, not Raggedy Ann and Andy. You're marrying each other, which is great, but that doesn't mean you're in for a lifetime of color coordinating your clothes. Matching was good for the prom, but for your wedding, it's time to move on.

THE STUDS should coordinate with your cuff links. They can be sterling silver, onyx, lapis, or inexpensive silk knots. Studs really finish the whole look off. You don't want to go too crazy with studs or you'll look like Liberace. Think simple, demure, understated. No one should be able to see your studs from across the room.

THE TIE: Lately you've probably seen lots of celebrities pairing tuxedos with long ties, and that can look very handsome. But for the average guy, keeping it as simple and classic as possible is always the right answer, so I recommend a bow tie with a tux. You'll just never be wrong.

I'm talking about a black grosgrain bow tie that you've tied yourself. A premade bow tie only tells the world of your secret desire to be a catering waiter. It just screams rented. You can wear the most expensive, glorious, custom-made tuxedo, but if you slap on a clip-on bow tie, you might as well tape a sign on your head that says LOSER. Oh, and the tie is *black*, folks. Colored ties might have worked for your prom, but so did that Flock of Seagulls haircut. Would Cary Grant wear a dusty rose or burgundy bow tie? I think, um, *knot*.

THE VEST: Personally, I think a vest is unnecessary. It's not improper, but when we think about tuxedos, we should think about those role models who've worn them so well: men like Cary Grant and the cast of *Ocean's Eleven*. And that means just a clean, sophisticated tuxedo with white shirt, black tie, and black cummerbund. Any time it gets tricky with vests or whatever, you could very easily look like you're going to the prom on *Beverly Hills 90210*. And we don't want Shannen Doherty on our bad side, now do we?

THE POCKET SQUARE is white silk. Simple enough.

THE CUMMERBUND, like the tie, is also made of grosgrain, and the pleats go facing up. That's because they were originally meant to catch crumbs or hold opera tickets. Oh, and by the way? There's only one b in "cummerbund" people. It's Cum. Mer. Bund. Now, is that so hard to remember? (Isn't that naughty?)

BRACES: I really like braces with a tux. (And I prefer the British term—braces—which seems more elegant and formal, and refers to something that buttons on the back of your pants.) Since you're not wearing a belt, if your tuxedo pants don't fit perfectly, you may want to wear braces. It's the one part of a tuxedo that you can actually have a little fun with, because braces will often have patterns woven into them, much like a novelty tie. Like wedding food, let's just hope it's tasteful.

THE CUFF LINKS should coordinate with the studs. Understated is fine, or you could get nutty and choose larger, more conspicuous cuff links. They could even be a little whimsical: hot and cold water faucets, horseshoes, whatever. Anything but a cartoon character, really.

THE PANTS are flat-front with stripes down the sides made of satin or grosgrain that matches the trim on the lapels. That stripe is known as a satin braid, but it's not actually a braid. Go figure. It's one of life's great mysteries. That and Stonehenge.

THE SOCKS are black silk dress socks. They will feel like women's panty hose. I know you'll pretend not to like it. But secretly, inside, you do!

THE SHOES are patent leather lace-up dress shoes. Velvet slippers if you absolutely must. (See chapter one.)

If you go to more than three or four formal events a year, you can have a little fun and switch things up. Maybe you throw in a fun scarf, or different cuff links or sophisticated braces, but this is not for amateurs.

If you have more than one tux, you can throw a white dinner jacket into the mix. They're stylish and chic, in that very Rock Hudson/Cary Grant/James Dean kind of way. If you really want to be daring, try a colored dinner jacket. I have a beautiful pink tropical-weight wool dinner jacket I wore to the Golden Globes. But for the one-tuxedo guy, black and classic it is. I'm queer, are you clear?

When You Wear Tux

Tuxedos are worn to formal events held after six o'clock in the evening. If you get an invitation for a black tie event before six, send me the names of the hosts. I'll "shoot 'em an e-mail." Or I'll just shoot 'em.

If the invitation says "black tie optional," you can wear a dark suit with a tie, but you run the risk of looking like somebody's security detail. Sure, it's technically proper to wear a suit, but everyone might look at you and wonder, "Who's the loser who doesn't own a tuxedo?"

I don't get "black tie preferred," either. It's either black tie or it's not. Give people some direction, for God's sake. If black tie is "preferred" and you show up in a dark suit, does that mean you won't get the best hors d'oeuvres or something?

And if the invitation says "creative black tie," ugh! Those are three words that need to be eradicated. Black tie is just not a place to get creative. Let's leave that to Fantasy Thursdays in the privacy of your own bedroom.

FOR THE SEASON

DRESSING

When it comes to dressing appropriately for the season, there are certain hard and fast (giggle) rules you need to follow. I've covered these already, but it can't hurt to reiterate them. No wearing white after Labor Day. Linen is for spring and summer unless you live in southern California or Florida. You only wear flannel in fall and winter, and I'm talking about gray flannel trousers, not Paul Bunyan flannel work-shirts, which you shouldn't be wearing *ever*. Open-toed shoes like sandals and flip-flops are only worn from Memorial Day through Labor Day, please. Seersucker is strictly summer only. And white Cadillacs? Never.

For anything beyond that, it's simply a question of "are you comfortable?" You shouldn't be wearing a cashmere turtleneck in August, unless you're in the southern hemisphere. Global warming notwithstanding, you shouldn't be wearing Bermuda shorts in Manhattan in the middle of January. That's just basic common sense, kids.

IS YOUR DREAMCATCHER? FINDING YOUR COLORS

WHAT COLOR

I always thought people just "got" it when it came to knowing what colors looked good on them. Until I started dressing clueless straight men for a living. I would say, "Why wouldn't you wear this color?" And they'd say, "Oh, I don't know."

Color is so personal and there is so much out there—just experiment with it. I'm not going to force you to go have your color analysis done. (I'm a summer, by the way.) But it's really true that there are basic concepts to guide you. Avoid colors of 1970s appliances given away on *The Price Is Right*—you know, harvest gold and avocado. That should keep you out of trouble. And be especially careful about the colors you put around your face. If you have fair skin and you wear very bright colors, the clothes are going to suck the color right out of you. Looking like you have jaundice is so rarely the right answer.

fair complexion   medium complexion   dark complexion

Here's a handy guide to get you started on color basics. People with fair skin, light hair, blue eyes, and soft features (You know, cute, like me!) look great in soft pastels: pale pink, pale blue, ivory, lavender. We don't always look good in black. Don't be afraid of pastels. Remember, wearing pink doesn't make you gay. And if you have blue eyes, wearing bright blues just intensifies them. It's the next best thing to getting laid.

If you're one of our dark and swarthy friends—mmmm, my favorite!—and have strong features, you generally look great in strong colors: black, chocolate brown, warm orange, aubergine (that's French for eggplant!). The darker your skin, the more you can get away with wearing those bright reds and yellows and oranges.

What if you're stuck in the middle, with mousy brown hair and medium-tone skin? Life's not so bad, my friend! Put those pills down. You can wear any color under the sun, including those yummy muted earth tones like English khaki, taupe, and my favorite, loden green.

DRESSING FOR YOUR BODY TYPE

Just like finding your colors, dressing for your body type is so very personal. God made you unique, just like everybody else! You have to experiment to see what works best for your body's proportions and shapes. If you're shaped like a pear, you've got bigger problems than knowing what to wear.

All this mumbo jumbo about what you should do for a round face, square face, etc., is preposterous. Everybody's shaped differently—like snowflakes! You're really going to have to experiment. Contrary to what most people say, unless you're rocking a body like Jabba the Hutt, loose-fitting clothes are rarely the right answer. But you don't want to look like a human hot dog, either. You just want clothes that fit your body.

One good general rule, though, is that if you're on the large side, you should wear more subdued colors and patterns. Because when viewing them, your eye doesn't

patterns can make
you look huge

monochromatic solids
are slimming

have a reference point as to scale. If I see a large man wearing a rose print, and I can count at least a hundred roses on his shirt, I know enough to hide my Twinkies. If he's wearing just black, my eye doesn't have anything to compare it to, so he'll look more proportionate and less overwhelming.

"Twisted"

Here are some fun alternatives to old standbys:

Instead of a pocket square, use a faded blue bandanna.

Instead of a sweater under a blazer, try a denim jacket.

Instead of dress shoes with a suit, try a Chelsea boot.

Instead of penny loafers with khakis and a blue blazer, try flip-flops.

Urbane

Cowboy

from Carson's Closet

10

Let's Make Fashion Happen, People!

FINDING INSPIRATION . . . AND FINDING GREAT CLOTHES

Attitude—Be Like Winona and Carry It Off

When you've finally found your personal style, having the right attitude and confidence will be the cherry on top of the proverbial sundae.

So how do you get there? Well, it helps to be inspired. And that doesn't mean you have to watch the Style network twenty-four hours a day or jet off to Milan twice a year for fashion week. (See sidebar, below.) It could mean going to museums, where you might see a painting that has certain colors that appeal to you. You might see the interior of a high-end car—and the leather and piping might inspire you to buy a cool leather jacket. It could mean buying the Italian fashion magazine *L'Uomo Vogue* once a year, which is the *Sports Illustrated* Swimsuit Edition of clothing. It could be looking through a book about motorcycles and seeing pictures of authentic motorcycle gear. All those things are inspiring. I'm not saying you're going to put on a whole head-to-toe motorcycle getup, because you'll look like some jackass NASCAR mascot. But something you see might inspire you to take your style to the next level, to put it in a new light and really have fun. *That,* and not the Hokey Pokey, is what it's all about.

It also helps to have a fashion role model who already has it all together. You know, like me! Start looking around. The world is filled with great sources of fashion inspi-

A Word of Caution About Fashion Shows

Fashion shows are put on by designers as the height of fantasy and high concept. Just like art shows, they're meant to showcase signature pieces that make a statement and show a designer's point of view for that particular season. They're meant to generate buzz and excitement, not to show you clothes you would actually go to the mall in Peoria to buy.

Here's a comparison I know you'll understand: Fashion shows are like auto shows. You don't go to the auto show expecting that the next week you're going to buy the $300,000 prototype Bentley Azure you saw. You go there to see what's out there, to have fun, to be entertained, and most importantly to be inspired. You may not drive off with the Bentley, but you might go and buy the new Toyota Celica, which has some of those elements and features to which you reacted.

So when you see that $3500 cashmere-and-goat-suede jacket in a fashion show or high-end fashion magazine—you know, the one that can only be cleaned with Alaskan Malamute dog urine—it's not that you're supposed to buy that exact jacket. But six months later, in H&M, you might find a more palatable, watered-down version of it in faux shearling for $150. The touch, the color, the feel of it might be similarly styled. That, my straight friends, is what we call being inspired. It's not about fashion. It's about personal style and about looking good.

ration. One great resource is your local Blockbuster. No, not the uniform, silly. Movies are full of men whose style is worth emulating—Cary Grant, James Dean, Steve McQueen, Pierce Brosnan. Rent the original *Thomas Crown Affair* and see what Steve McQueen could do with a blue blazer. Rent *Ocean's Eleven* and see how a tuxedo should be worn. Rent *On the Waterfront* or *Rebel Without a Cause* (or *Grease!*) and see why a classic motorcycle jacket is always the right answer. Rent *The Adventures of Priscilla, Queen of the Desert*, just for giggles!

Or just go to the record store. Look at Lenny Kravitz or Tim McGraw and see how they pull together a look that works for them. Think about what they're wearing, why it looks cool, and what about it might inspire you. Once again, I'm not talking about copying an outfit down to the exact number of wrinkles in the socks; I'm talking about using that outfit to spark something, to stir something deep within you. A fashion chubby, if you will.

News flash: Buying fashion magazines doesn't make you gay. Wallpapering your bedroom with the Abercrombie & Fitch catalog makes you gay. If you were looking to invest in a new car, you'd go out and buy *Motor Trend* to get some ideas, wouldn't you? If you're going to invest in a suit or a new fall wardrobe, you should do the same thing: Buy yourself a copy of *GQ, Esquire*, or *Cargo*. Pay attention to details. Tear out pages with looks that you like. If you're not confident enough to go out and get them on your own, build a relationship with a salesperson you trust at a store with a good reputation. Bring the salesperson the tear sheets and say, "Do you have something like this?" or "Where can I find this?" and he or she will be happy to help you. That person will want your repeat business and won't steer you in the wrong direction.

Shopping: Hunting and Fishing for Fashion

The road to fabulosity can be a long and arduous—but ultimately satisfying—journey. It might, however, involve some shopping. And a lot of straight men—egads!—just don't like to shop.

Why not? In our culture, it's women, not men, who are taught to do the shopping. They go grocery shopping, they go clothes shopping, and they learn how to navigate the retail landscape of this great land of ours. So they are just more comfortable with it and efficient at it. If you had no idea how to operate a car and were asked to get on I-95, you would be petrified, too.

Shopping is uncharted territory for a lot of men, a place where they feel uneducated. And we all know men don't like being out of control. It's straight out of *Men Are from Mars, Women Are from Venus*. Men like things to be organized and in order. And nowadays shopping is not organized and well ordered. Department stores are crazy and the Internet is huge. It seems very chaotic, and men don't like that. They don't have the vocabulary and the training to articulate what they're looking for and find it efficiently.

What Makes a Classic?

A classic is an icon. It's something that always looks good on everyone. A classic two-button blue blazer looks good on almost everybody because of its silhouette, how it's made, and the materials. Same goes for cowboy boots, Levi's 501s, and Ray-Bans. But you don't even have to look to clothes for inspiration—beautiful design can be found in everyday objects.

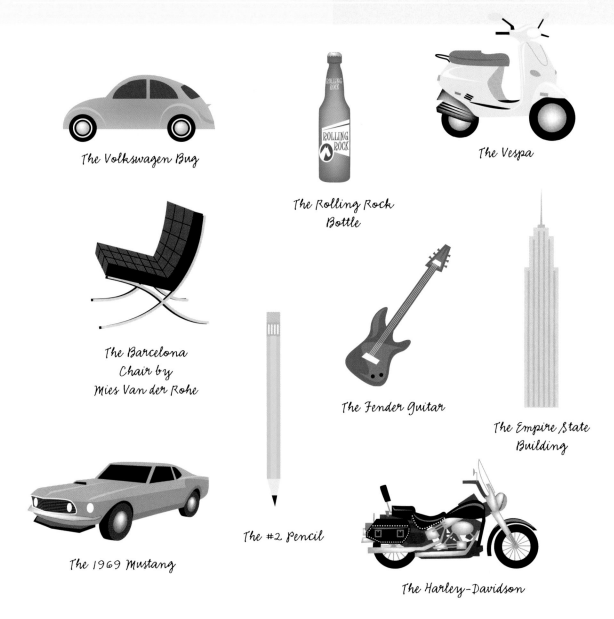

The Volkswagen Bug

The Rolling Rock Bottle

The Vespa

The Barcelona Chair by Mies Van der Rohe

The Fender Guitar

The Empire State Building

The 1969 Mustang

The #2 Pencil

The Harley-Davidson

Polaroiding (Not for Amateurs)

In one of my favorite films of all time, *Clueless*, the main character, Cher, would always take a friend shopping with her so the friend could take a Polaroid of her in each outfit. It's something we did when I worked fashion shows, too. If you want, you can photograph outfits that look great on you so you can remember how to reconstruct them. I would suggest you do this only if it's a special wardrobe item that you don't wear very often—like your favorite wedding suit/shirt/tie combo. If it's an all-time favorite, yeah, go ahead and take a photo of it and keep it in your underwear drawer. A meddling girlfriend can break up with you over it. Let me repeat: This is not for amateurs or the average guy. Honestly, who is going to have the time?

The ironic thing for me is that so many straight men hate shopping, but they can sit in trees all day waiting for a deer to scamper across their path and shoot it. Shopping is like hunting or sports: You've got a goal. You've got a barrier. (Bad credit!) You've got people on your team. You've got opponents. You've got coaches. You've got cheerleaders—well, one, that's me. What, you didn't recognize me with the pom-poms? You've got men in tight spandex pants. Well, maybe if you go to Barneys you'll see a couple. But they're not on your team, they're on mine.

Anyway, if you know how to navigate the system, shopping is much easier and quicker and you get better results. It doesn't have to be painful. It can be fun, enjoyable, and productive, it can save you money, and it can make you look better. Best of all, you can have lunch while you're at it. So let's empower you to be a better shopper, shall we?

Shopping in five easy steps:

1. **Never shop alone.** You want to be with someone who can provide you with an honest opinion, someone who will tell you straight out if the clothes are not right for you, if the color is off, or if something doesn't fit correctly. So take your significant other or a friend. If you don't have any friends, that's sad. But just try to get a second opinion: A fairy godstylist at your favorite clothing store, or another gay man, can tell you if things look good or not. And whether you're alone or not, before you buy anything, check yourself in a three-way mirror.

2. **Go out and practice.** This shopping thing isn't easy. It takes a lot of hard work and practice. Do an experiment: Go shopping for a day and resolve not to buy anything. Just see what's out there. It gives you some education and helps to keep you from making impulse purchases that you might regret.

3. **Shop for who you are now and not who you will be five pounds from now.** But on the flip side, don't be afraid to try different silhouettes and experiment with looks outside your comfort zone.

4. **Mix it up.** There are so many places to get a wardrobe together, from Target, T.J.Maxx, and Marshalls to Barneys and Neiman Marcus. They all have great things and oftentimes the more interesting looks come from mixing and matching. Don't forget the Internet. There's a vast world of clothing available to you by just browsing. And then you don't even have to leave home!

5. **Don't become a sale slut.** You shouldn't buy stuff just because it's inexpensive or on sale. If you don't ever wear that sale item, or you have to dispose of it wearing a hazmat suit, it's not a bargain.

Don't Ask, Don't Tell: Carson's Secrets of Bargain Shopping

Looking good is not about the price tag. But I won't lie: Shopping on a shoestring is not as easy as shopping on an endless budget; you just have to be smart about it.

Here's my theory about bargain shopping. You can find deals in any area of your wardrobe. If you want a bargain suit or shoes, you can find them. But I'd rather see you buy good quality brands and materials, even if you have to hunt for them on sale, rather than buy cheap things at full retail.

If you've got the time—perhaps you're unemployed and have nothing else to fill up your day—you can dig around and find good things almost anywhere, even at those cheesy mall stores with shiny double-breasted lavender suits in the window. But in my opinion, you would be better served to go to a store where you know they have clothes that are well constructed, well made, and flattering. Finding bargains

can sometimes be a little bit like a scavenger hunt, and you have to be more of an expert to know what you're looking for. You're going to spend less money, but you're also going to spend more time and effort looking. The luxury of spending more money is that it doesn't take as much time to walk into a place like Bergdorf Goodman and say, "I'll take that, that and, oh!, that." Money for time is a totally viable trade-off. God, I sound like an economics major.

There are some stores with a reputation for having good quality clothes at seriously discounted prices: national chains like T.J.Maxx, Marshalls, Filene's, Loehmann's, or New York's gem, Century 21. Here are three quick tips for shopping at places like these:

1. Go early in the day, when the store is organized and the merchandise is fresh.

2. Shop when you have time and won't be distracted.

3. Be mindful of final-sale items that cannot be returned.

Another great resource not to be overlooked is consignment shops and resale places, where they have designer clothing that may be a season or two old. Shhh! No one's going to know. You can get a great deal, like a Gucci jacket half off. They're only lightly worn. Don't worry. You won't find Monica Lewinsky's blue dress. That's over at the Gap world headquarters.

Thrift stores can also be a gold mine—as much as it pains me to use the word thrift. Just know that there's a difference between *vintage* clothing and *thrift*. At a thrift store like a Goodwill, you're going to have to wade through mounds of skanky clothing to find those hidden treasures. But at a more upscale vintage clothing store, they've

What's in a name?

You might be surprised to hear this coming from me, but it's not that important that your clothes bear a designer label. What's most important is the look, fit, and quality of the clothes. The designer label isn't important in and of itself, but it can help clue you in to a lot of information about construction and quality before you make the purchase. You might know a designer whose clothes have a reputation for being super high quality that lasts forever. Or maybe you know a designer who makes good quality, inexpensive clothes that are meant to be thrown out after a season. Either way, that's useful information.

Designer labels do represent reputation, quality, and commitment to design excellence. So don't be fooled by cheap imposters. Giorgio Mymommy and Dolce and Garbanzo are not what they're pretending to be. Polo with two *l*'s? That's chicken, people. Think of it like a car. A brand has a heritage and tradition of quality and a benchmark that they set to maintain their customer base. Would you buy a car called a Dyslexus and expect it to perform like a Lexus just because the name was similar? I think ton. I mean not.

POLLO

DOLCE & GARBANZO

If you see new "designer" clothing at a flea market or being sold on the street by a guy also selling glowsticks and Yankees tickets, hello! It's not the real deal. Someone like me can spot fakes a mile away because the silhouette is off—it's big and boxy rather than trim and tailored. Or the fabric is different; it's hard like sandpaper rather than soft and supple. Or the logo is the wrong size. My favorite is "Knights of the Round Table," which is a Polo knockoff. Instead of a horse and polo player, they have a horse and jouster. Nice try, people. This is *not* my first day at the Renaissance Faire.

already waded through the junk and narrowed it down for you. Obviously prices will be higher at a vintage store than at a thrift store.

Regardless of the store, you want to really look at construction and fabric content, because there are some really cool designs from the fifties, sixties, and seventies. However, this was the heyday of Dacron, so beware of clothes that seem to be made of old lawn furniture. Look for things that are real cotton, silk, or wool, and

A Cheat Sheet for Brands

These brands all tend to be very consistent. You're buying peace of mind that you're going to get consistent quality at various price points.

- Abercrombie & Fitch
- Armani
- Banana Republic
- Barneys
- Bloomingdales
- Hugo Boss
- Calvin Klein
- Club Monaco

- Diesel
- DKNY
- Dolce & Gabbana
- Etro
- The Gap
- Gucci
- H&M
- Tommy Hilfiger

- Levi's
- Nautica
- Neiman Marcus
- Nordstrom
- Old Navy
- Polo Ralph Lauren
- Saks Fifth Avenue
- John Varvatos

try everything on because sizing and fit in earlier eras were very different from today. A small in 1970 does not a small in 2004 make.

And lastly, the most important piece of advice: Wash it, wash it, and wash it again. Clothing can host mold and mildew and harbor all kinds of strange and mysterious odors. If you wash it with one cup of white vinegar, it will remove some of that thrift-store fragrance—you know, the one that smells like old-lady feet or the interior of a 1974 Dodge Dart.

EPILOGUE

NOW THAT YOU'VE GOTTEN THIS FAR, I BET YOU'RE WONDERING, "CARSON, JUST WHAT WOULD THE WORLD LOOK LIKE IF STRAIGHT men were good little lambs and followed your fashion advice?"

Well, people, it would be a beautiful thing. The world would look like everyone was a sales associate at Neiman Marcus. No, wait, that could be hellish. Scratch that.

It would be a yummy world of color and cashmere, of friendly hellos and twinkles in the eye from knowing we all looked and felt our best. Every man would find a style that worked for him and wouldn't be afraid to embrace who he really is, even if it meant wearing stripes in a paisley world. The GNP would soar, and we'd all be like one big Benetton ad, with everybody united in peace, harmony, and couture.

It would be a world without hockey jerseys, except on hockey players. (But they would fit tighter!) Sweatpants hiked up to your knees would be eradicated. White Reebok hightops would be banished, never to be seen again. Mock turtlenecks would be a thing of the past. Little children would say things like "What is this mock turtle-neck you speak of, Father?" or "Daddy, tell me again about the olden days of yore when people used to wear Coogi sweaters and Cavariccis." And the answer would come. "Oh, son, that was a long, long time ago and the world was a dark, scary, ugly, evil place. But then along came a fairy godstylist named Carson Kressley, and he changed all of that . . ."

But then things get all blurry and I wake up in a sweat, thrashing about in my thousand-thread-count Pratesi sheets, giving my hair even more split ends. It was only a dream.

But it doesn't have to be. You can make it a reality. So I leave you with these parting words of wisdom: Go. Shop. Grab lunch. Cuddle.

Together we can make the world a beautiful place.

Hugs and Cashmere,